HIDDEN GALLERIES

MATERIAL RELIGION IN THE SECRET POLICE ARCHIVES IN CENTRAL AND EASTERN EUROPE

EDITED BY

James Kapaló and Tatiana Vagramenko

LIT

ANTHROPOLOGY OF RELIGION / RELIGIONSETHNOLOGIE
Band / Volume 3

This book is printed on acid-free paper.

Bibliographic information published by the Deutsche Nationalbibliothek
The Deutsche Nationalbibliothek lists this publication in the Deutsche Nationalbibliografie; detailed bibliographic data are available in the Internet at http://dnb.dnb.de.
ISBN 978-3-643-91263-3 (pb)
ISBN 978-3-643-96263-8 (PDF)

A catalogue record for this book is available from the British Library.

Flössergasse 10
CH-8001 Zürich
Tel. +41 (0) 76-632 84 35
E-Mail: zuerich@lit-verlag.ch http://www.lit-verlag.ch

Distribution:
In the UK: Global Book Marketing, e-mail: mo@centralbooks.com
In North America: Independent Publishers Group, e-mail: orders@ipgbook.com
In Germany: LIT Verlag Fresnostr. 2, D-48159 Münster
Tel. +49 (0) 2 51-620 32 22, Fax +49 (0) 2 51-922 60 99, e-mail: vertrieb@lit-verlag.de

---o0o---

This project has received funding from the European Research Council (ERC) under the European Union's Horizon 2020 research and innovation programme No. 677355.

We dedicate this book to
the memory of all those whose voices and faces
were buried deep within the secret police archives,
never meant to be seen or heard from again

CONTENTS

CONTRIBUTORS

Iuliana Cindrea has an MA from the Department of History, Patrimony and Protestant Theology at Lucian Blaga University, Sibiu, Romania. She is currently a PhD candidate in the Study of Religions Department at University College Cork on the Hidden Galleries project. Her main research interests include the history of religious minorities in Romania, the manner in which they were perceived by totalitarian regimes in the twentieth century and the repressive mechanisms used by the state. The title of her PhD research is *Hidden Galleries, Silenced Communities: Religious Minorities and the Secret Police in twentieth Century Romania*.

Ágnes Hesz is assistant lecturer at the Department of European Ethnology–Cultural Anthropology, University of Pécs, Hungary. Her main research interests are vernacular religion, everyday religious practice under socialism, cultures of death and contemporary discourses on witchcraft. She is the author of *Élők, holtak és adósságok. A halottak szerepe egy erdélyi faluközösségben* [The Dead, the Living and their Debts: The Role of the Dead in a Village Community] (Budapest: L'Harmattan, 2012).

James Kapaló is senior lecturer in the Study of Religions at University College Cork, Ireland and co-director of the Marginalized and Endangered Worldviews Study Centre (MEWSC). He is author of two monographs, *Text, Context and Performance: Gagauz Folk Religion in Discourse and Practice* (Leiden: Brill, 2008) and *Inochentism and Orthodox Christianity: Religious Dissent in the Russian and Romanian Borderlands* (Routledge: London, 2019), as well as several journal articles and book chapters. He is the Principal Investigator of the Hidden Galleries ERC project.

Dumitru Lisnic holds an MA degree in history from the Alexandru Ioan Cuza University of Iași, Romania. He participated in research projects focused on collectivization of agriculture under communism and Romanian POWs detained in NKVD camps, and conducted research on local elites in post-war Moldavian SSR. Currently he is PhD candidate at the Department of the Study of Religions at University College Cork. His main research interests include the history of the Soviet Union and ethno-religious minorities in Eastern Europe. The title of his PhD research at UCC is *Policing the Margins: Repression, Propaganda and Religious Minorities in Soviet Moldavia in the 1920s–1930s*.

Gabriela Nicolescu has a PhD in visual anthropology from Goldsmiths, University of London. She has taught anthropology of art, museum studies and medical, economic and political anthropology from material and visual perspectives at Goldsmiths and the University of Bucharest. From October 2018 to January 2020 she was the curatorial lead of the Hidden Galleries project at University College Cork. Currently she is a postdoctoral researcher at the School of Anthropology and Museum Ethnography, University of Oxford. For access to her recent publications and curated exhibitions, please visit http://gabrielanicolescu.com/.

Kinga Povedák has a PhD in European Ethnology from the University of Szeged, Hungary. Currently she is research fellow at the "Convivence" Religious Pluralism Research Group (Hungarian Academy of Sciences–University of Szeged). Her recent publications explore vernacular religiosity during socialist Hungary, Christianity and popular culture, and Pentecostal charismatic Christianity. She is the author of *Gitáros Apostolok. A keresztény könnyűzene vallástudományi vizsgálata* [Guitarist Apostles: The study of Christian popular music] (Szeged: MTA-SZTE Vallási Kultúrakutató Csoport, 2019).

Anca Șincan has a PhD in history from Central European University. She teaches courses at the History and International Relations Department at George Emil Palade University of Medicine, Pharmacy, Science and Technology of Tîrgu-Mureș and is researcher at the Gheorghe Șincai Institute for Social Sciences and Humanities of the Romanian Academy in Tîrgu-Mureș. Her research interests revolve around the recent history of East Central Europe, the history of historical writing, memory and remembrance, church history, religion and politics, on which she has published articles and book chapters. She took part as an expert in the Presidential Commission for the Study of the Communist Dictatorship in Romania.

Tatiana Vagramenko has a PhD in anthropology from National University of Ireland, Maynooth. She is a postdoctoral researcher at University College Cork, Ireland and a George F. Kennan Fellow at the Woodrow Wilson International Center for Scholars, Washington, DC. Her project, *Religious Minorities in Ukraine from the Soviet Underground to the Euromaidan: Pathways to Religious Freedom and Pluralism in Enlarging Europe*, funded by the Irish Research Council, explores historical materials from recently opened KGB archives in Ukraine and the ethnography of the Euromaidan Revolution.

---o0o---

ACKNOWLEDGEMENTS

This book constitutes one of the key outputs of the European Research Council project *Creative Agency and Religious Minorities: "Hidden Galleries" in the Secret Police Archives in Central and Eastern Europe* and is based on materials included in the Hidden Galleries Digital Archive (http://hiddengalleries.eu/digitalarchive/) and the subsequent public exhibitions. The Ukrainian materials in this collection come from the research project *Religious Minorities in Ukraine from the Soviet Underground to the Euromaidan: Pathways to Religious Freedom and Pluralism in Enlarging Europe*, funded by the Irish Research Council. We would also like to thank the COST Action *New Exploratory Phase in Research on East European Cultures of Dissent* (CA 16213) for their collaboration in completing this research.

We are extremely grateful to Gabriela Nicolescu, whose curatorial work on the Hidden Galleries exhibitions has helped shape this book and the materials presented within it. The writing and editing of the labels for the Hidden Galleries exhibitions by the curators along with the editors and authors of this book have helped make this a truly collaborative work. Special thanks also go to Dr. Igor Cașu, who was instrumental in helping the project gain access to materials in Moldova as well as giving inspiration and offering ideas in the early stages of the project; and to Siobhán O'Brien, our Research Support Officer, who has ensured the smooth running of so many aspects of this project throughout its four years.

This project would not have been possible without the close collaboration and help we received from the archival institutions in Romania, Hungary, the Republic of Moldova and Ukraine. In particular, we would like to thank Cseh Gergő Bendegúz, Director of the Historical Archives of the Hungarian State Security (Állambiztonsági Szolgálatok Történeti Levéltára–ÁBTL) for his enthusiastic support and for hosting the first project workshop at ÁBTL in September 2017 and all the staff there for their ongoing help in locating and accessing archival materials. We also owe an enormous debt of gratitude to the staff at the National Council for the Study of the Securitate Archives (Consiliul Național pentru Studierea Arhivelor Securității–CNSAS). The support of the successive directors of CNSAS, Dragoș Petrescu and Constantin Buchet, and of Silviu Moldovan, Head of Research, was invaluable in realizing our vision for this publication and the project more broadly. Special thanks also go to Andriy Kohut, the director of the State Archive Branch of the Security Services of Ukraine (Haluzevyi derzhavnyi arkhiv Sluzhby bezpeky Ukrainy–HDA SBU), and archivist Maria Panova, who facilitated the access to Ukrainian materials.

Our sincere thanks go to members of the faith communities whose images and materials appear here. Many of them gave generously their time to meet with us, answer our questions and offer their insights and suggestions. In no particular order our thanks go to the Monastery of the Dormition of the Mother of God of the Romanian Orthodox Church of the Old Style, Bucharest (Mănăstirea Adormirea Maicii Domnului a Bisericii Ortodoxe Române de Stil Vechi din București); the Monastery of the Refuge of the Mother of God of the Romanian Orthodox Church of the Old Style, Selimbar (Mănăstirea Acoperământul Maicii Domnului a Bisericii Ortodoxe Române de Stil Vechi din Șelimbăr); the Monastery of the Annunciation of the Romanian Orthodox Church of the Old Calendar, Valea Roșie (Mănăstirea Ortodoxă de Stil Vechi Buna Vestire, Valea Roșie); believers of the Greek Catholic community form Băița, Mureș county, Romania; the Tudorist community, Romania; the Hungarian Reformed Choir in Ocna Sibiului, Romania; Pastor Lilla Gere from Budapest; and the Inochentist community from Balta, Ukraine.

In the realization of the Digital Archive, we received invaluable advice from Orla Murphy, Jessie Labov and Jennifer Edmund. Jamie Furey deserves a special thank you for his tenacity and ingenuity in solving the many technical issues that arose with the archive.

Following on from the archival and ethnographic fieldwork, the project team also mounted a series of public exhibitions staged in 2019 and 2020. The project team is indebted to the following people and institutions, who offered their support and collaboration in the staging of the exhibitions: Lucian Nastasă-Kovacs and Alexandra Sârbu from the Museum of Art in Cluj-Napoca (Romania); Katalin Székely from the Open Society Archives Gallery in Budapest (Hungary); Petru Vicol, Teodor Candu and Andrei Prohin from the Museum of Ethnography and Natural History in Chișinău (Moldova); Cronán ó Doibhlin of University College Cork Library (Ireland) and to Alexandru Bud of the Central University Library "Lucian Blaga" in Cluj-Napoca for hosting our special display there. Thank you also to Lauren Winton and Michael Lawrence at Bladud Flies! for the visual design work and sound at the Cluj-Napoca exhibition and for the creative work on this volume and to Daniel Kophelyi for designing the Budapest exhibition, to Roland Vaczi for the photographs that appear in this book from the opening of the exhibition in Cluj-Napoca, and to Patty Gray for her meticulous work as copyeditor of this catalogue.

Finally, we would also like to thank the following individuals for their support, advice and inspiration during the course of the project: Lavinia Stan, Cristina Vățulescu, Dorin Lozovanu, Éva Petrás, Szilvia Köbel, Alexandra Djuric-Milovanovic, Lana Peternel, Gasper Mithans, Muriel Blaive, Roland Clark, Corneliu Pintilescu, Iemima Ploscariu, Helena Buffery, Lidia Guzy, Árpád Szakolczai, Anthony Muldoon, Catherine Wanner and Katherine Furman.

---oOo---

LIST OF ARCHIVES

This book features materials from the following institutions and private collections:

National Council for the Study of the Securitate Archives (Consiliul Național pentru Studierea Arhivelor Securității–CNSAS)

National Archives of Romania (Arhivele Naționale ale României–ANR)

Historical Archives of the Hungarian State Security (Állambiztonsági Szolgálatok Történeti Levéltára–ÁBTL)

National Archives of the Republic of Moldova (Arhiva Națională a Republicii Moldova–ANRM)

Archives of the Information and Security Services of the Republic of Moldova (Arhiva Serviciului de Informații și Securitate al Republicii Moldova–ASISRM)

State Archive Branch of the Security Services of Ukraine (Haluzevyi derzhavnyi arkhiv Sluzhby bezpeky Ukrainy–HDA SBU)

Archive of the SBU in Chernivetska Oblast (Sektor arkhivnoho zabezpechennia USBU v Chernivets'kii oblasti–SAZ USBU Chernivetska obl.)

Private photo collection of Mihai and Ana Rus from Băița village, Mureș county

NOTE ON TRANSLITERATION

When rendering archival documents and references, we have followed the Library of Congress system of transliteration from Russian and Ukrainian, omitting diacritics. All place names are given in their recognizable international form, where such exist, for example: Bucharest, Kiev. All other place names are given in their standard local contemporary form. In the case of Ukraine, place names have been transliterated from Ukrainian (Kharkiv, Bila Tserkva). Ukrainian individual names usually appear in their Russian forms in the Soviet-era archival sources, but for the purposes of this publication, they have been transliterated from Ukrainian.

INTRODUCTION

ARCHIVES AND FAITH COMMUNITIES

James Kapaló and Tatiana Vagramenko

During the twentieth century, some states in Central and Eastern Europe attempted to eliminate religious groups that were deemed dangerous or undesirable. Communist regimes pursued this policy with the aim of creating atheist societies free from religious influences whilst right-wing dictatorships targeted minority religious groups with the aim of homogenizing nation-states, often around the majority ethnic and religious identity. But a paradoxical thing happened: testimonies, photographs, personal and sacred items, and the ephemera of religious life were preserved by the very state institutions whose role it was to destroy them. The secret police played a pivotal role in these states' attempts to control and regulate the religious field, and their archives contain a rich collection of confiscated images, texts and items that were used to incriminate members of religious groups. Alongside these materials, the secret police produced their own representations of the communities they were tasked with surveilling and controlling. This book catalogues the ways in which totalitarian states tried to capture religion in images, graphics, texts and dossiers in order to control and eliminate those they deemed undesirable.

This collection grows out of the research project *Creative Agency and Religious Minorities: "Hidden Galleries" in the Secret Police Archives in Central and Eastern Europe*, funded by the European Research Council. The Hidden Galleries project aimed to uncover that which was hidden twice over—first by the religious groups who were forced underground, and second, by the secret police who found them and enclosed them in their archives. The materials presented here originate from the secret police and other state archives in Romania, Hungary, the Republic of Moldova and Ukraine. The citizens of these four countries shared a common experience of state repression and surveillance from the 1920s until the end of communism. Under both right-wing and left-wing dictatorships, religious difference or innovation became associated with enmity towards the state and in this context mainstream and majority religions also played a role in the repression of smaller and newer religious communities. In the 1930s and 1940s, as part of wide-ranging campaigns aimed at transforming the social order in the Soviet Union and under the nationalist regimes in Hungary and Romania, arrest, detention in labour camps and deportation became widespread means of dealing with banned religious groups and problematic religious leaders. During communism, periods of mass repression, which included the closure of many monasteries and places of worship of mainstream majority churches, including Orthodox, Catholic and others, deportations to the Gulag and forced labour camps (especially in the period from the 1920s to the early 1950s) were followed by the era of mass surveillance (roughly the late 1950s to the 1980s). In the Soviet Union, Stalin's short rapprochement with the Orthodox Church during the Second World War meant that most anti-religious operations and propaganda after this period were aimed at religious leaders and minority religious groups that were often western in origin, such as Jehovah's Witnesses or Adventists, and who were accused of being spies and collaborating with external powers. From the 1950s, the same was true in communist Romania and Hungary. As a KGB report from 1953 states, "illegal" religious groups were considered "harmful to the state by the very fact of their existence and the character of their activity."

In the era of mass surveillance, the secret police moved from overt violent repression, executions and deportations to subtler means of controlling and ridding society of dissenters. This included discrediting, denouncing, persuading, blackmailing and tempting with favours individuals they sought to control. In this work, the secret police recruited and relied on large numbers of informers, some highly trained and dedicated, others informal, irregular and unreliable, many of whom had often been coerced into collaborating. In Romania, the number of informers rose from 73,000 in 1968 to 144,289 in 1989.[1] The task was even more complicated, as officially believers could not be persecuted directly for their religious beliefs, as was the case of the Soviet Union, where on paper the constitution granted religious freedom. The infamous article 58 of the Soviet penal code on "Anti-Soviet Agitation and Propaganda" was one of the most commonly used charges against religious believers. Penal cases tended to be based on fabricated or exaggerated charges that translated religious practices into extremist political activity. In the Soviet Union, the late 1950s also saw the return of extensive anti-religious propaganda campaigns that filled newspapers, magazines and newsreels with stories of dangerous sectarians and charlatan priests.

Our selection of materials is not intended to present a history of the repression itself, but rather to illustrate how the secret police represented, visualized and systematized the groups that they were pursuing. The images and materials presented, which were all confiscated, collated or created by the police or secret police and originate from diverse, so-called anti-religious operations, have a dual character: they were used by the secret police as incriminating evidence against religious communities, which could also be utilized in propaganda campaigns; and they also represent the memory, cultural patrimony and creative spirit of these groups and individuals.

The archives paradoxically preserved these materials despite the regimes intention to eradicate the people, beliefs and cultures that produced them. Most of the materials you will find here, which represent a small fraction of the vast materials to be found in secret police and state archives, were located by a team of researchers who conducted archival research in the secret police and other state archives between 2016 and 2019. The team sifted through hundreds of thousands of pages of files in order to find these often uncatalogued, hidden visual and material traces of communities that had been targeted by the state. The images are of differing character, are of varied provenance and served diverse functions. However, once placed within the secret police archives, they were all submitted to an internal "bureaucratic logic of classification" that shaped the lives of religious believers.[2] Be they confiscated religious materials, personal notebooks, letters or surveillance photographs taken by a hidden camera, these materials were converted into the physical evidence of criminal activity of communities and believers. They entered a specific knowledge-generating space that constructed the religious other as politically dangerous and socially harmful. Our task as researchers was both to examine the logic of the production, curation and archival classification of visual and material religion in the secret police archives and to trace the original life of images and materials enclosed there back to their source communities.

The various archives have different regimes of access that impact who can read a file, when and under what circumstances. Rarely do members of the communities that were targeted know about their presence in the archives or how to gain access. Whenever possible, the researchers on the Hidden Galleries project approached individuals and communities in order to inform them of the existence of materials that relate to them and to discuss their experience of repression. In this book, we have included the stories and accounts of some of our encounters with individuals targeted by the state and with descendant communities. Connecting the archival past with the present lives of religious communities opened up a unique opportunity to hear believers' memories, their reflections on the personal and communal impact of surveillance, interrogations and house searches, and to hear stories that did not make it into the secret police archives or those that had been told in files that were later destroyed or disappeared. Our ethnographic work with communities enabled what Sonja Luehrmann refers to as an "oppositional reading" of such a biased, multi-layered and multi-voiced historical source

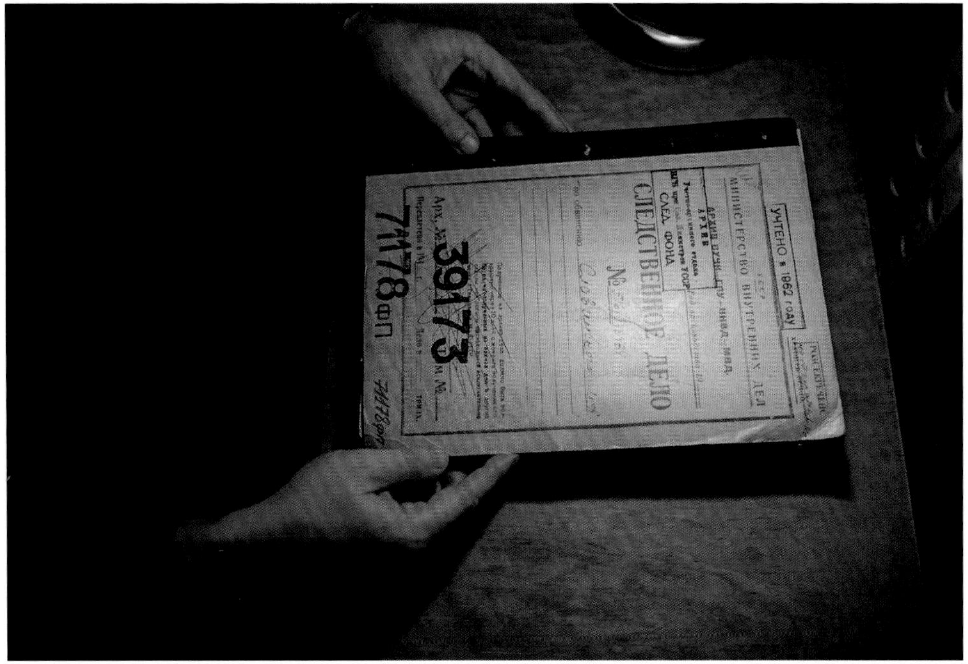

© Aleksei Filippov

[1] Lavinia Stan. *Transitional Justice in Post-Communist Romania: The Politics of Memory* (Cambridge University Press, 2013), 62.

[2] Sonja Luehrmann. *Religion in Secular Archives: Soviet Atheism and Historical Knowledge* (Oxford University Press, 2015), 4.

like the secret police archives.[3] A young girl who appeared in a confiscated photograph of her baptism learned nearly fifty years later that her image was preserved in the archives and was able to tell us the story of what happened to her community after the police raided their house church in 1972. A Tudorist pastor was able to see the first songbook produced by his community, which had been confiscated by the police many years earlier. A Hungarian Calvinist Church choir discovered that the documents, photographs and official stamp confiscated from them in the 1960s had been meticulously copied and compiled, by the secret police officer that stole them, into an impressive photo album. None of these confiscated items have been returned to these communities.

Secret police archives represent a problematic source for historians and researchers, from both an epistemological and ethical perspective. The overreliance on the texts they contain in the search for truth and justice in postcommunism has been the cause of numerous controversies due to the tendency to search them for black and white evidence of victimhood or collaboration, dissent or compliance. The ubiquitous fabrications, ideologically-driven misrepresentations and exaggerations make them unsuitable as stand-alone sources. The ethnographic approach taken by the Hidden Galleries project—starting with the visual and material religious presence in the archives, rather than the secret police's texts, and then working with faith communities—is designed to help overcome these ethical and interpretational dilemmas.

---oOo---

The images and materials in this collection are divided into four parts. The first part traces the variety of forms and appearances of what became known as the "religious underground." In order to escape the attention of the state and the eyes and ears of the secret police, some religious groups attempted to hide their activities, forming underground networks and clandestine communities. Such religious communities, however, were not solely the product of communist repression; many of them had come into existence earlier under the right-wing regimes that preceded them.

In some cases, religious communities chose to hide and worship in spaces dug underground, a practice that began before and continued during communism. Other groups chose to avoid detection by escaping to remote places to practice their beliefs, conducting services and rituals during hiking trips to the mountains or in forest hide-outs. Groups of ex-monks and ex-nuns, belonging to both Orthodox and Catholic traditions, who had been forced to give up their religious life when the state closed their monasteries, secretly set up house churches and communities. Some Evangelical, Pentecostal and Adventist groups who refused to accept oversight by the state also set up their own churches in their homes. But as the images you will see here show, the secret police were often able to uncover their hidden places of worship. Despite the attempts to evade surveillance, secret police officers managed to follow or infiltrate groups and to raid their clandestine places of worship, operations which were often captured on camera. In the Soviet Union, there was a close cooperation between the state security apparatus and public media. Images found in these files collected, produced and curated by the secret police were often later published in newspapers, in anti-religious teaching materials and in propaganda films.

The second part of this collection revolves around what Cristina Vățulescu refers to as police aesthetics.[4] Here we present the various forms of visual representation that the secret police employed in their information and evidence gathering operations. The graphics, maps, images and texts produced by the secret police about religious groups are the result of a distinct logic and set of practices. They served specific functions and were deployed in different contexts in order to fulfil their mission of gaining complete control over society through the gathering of information and the production of knowledge. These images also have a distinct aesthetic of their own, a police aesthetics. Photographs, whether produced by the secret police or confiscated and interpreted by officers, were the most common medium used to capture evidence and represent visually the targets of the state, from the simple mugshot to surveillance photographs, crime scene photographs and complex reconstructions involving whole photo albums. The photographic practices of the secret police were remarkably similar across Central and Eastern Europe and are all based on models and principles devised and taught by KGB officers.

The third part of the book presents examples of heretofore under-researched creative practices of religious movements under the oppressive regimes of the twentieth century. The creative visual and literary material represented here constitutes the lost or stolen cultural patrimony of repressed groups. The secret police were mostly interested in people, not in preserving objects and images, but inadvertently and paradoxically that is precisely what they have done. Unintentionally, they created the possibility for the personal artefacts and cultural patrimony of communities to experience a new life. Some of the materials you will see in the pages that follow are the result of confiscations, intrusive operations and the desecration of sacred places and objects that happened during the course of secret police operations. The personal photographs were created by the people themselves even though they were later used as weapons of incrimination. They show individuals and religious communities as they themselves wished to be portrayed, sometimes smiling and celebrating, at other times solemnly worshiping or mourning. Reflecting on these materials in particular, we may question whether they still belong in the archive or if they should be returned to communities. Unlike the texts written by the secret police, which have been mined for "facts" in the search for the truth about the repressive regimes of the past, the confiscated images and objects represent a very different legacy of the archives that can help tell other stories and histories.

The last section in this book is dedicated to reflections on the whole research process that led to this book, which was made complete by our engagement with, and contributions made by, our research participants. Many representatives of faith communities joined us at the opening of the project's first public exhibition titled *Hidden Galleries: Clandestine Religion in the Secret Police Archives* (Imagini din galerii secrete: religia clandestină în arhivele poliției secrete / Rejtett galériák: Az üldözött vallásosság képei a titkosszolgálati levéltárakban), which took place at the Museum of Art in Cluj-Napoca, Romania from 21 November to 29 December 2019. It was only when the research entered this final stage, when we were able to stand amongst the materials we had gathered together over three years, that the dispersed images and objects and the fragmented memories and precious stories eventually were rejoined. This is when the dusty archival folders and crumpled images truly came back to life as the faith communities themselves reconnected the broken threads of their past and voiced their views on their stolen patrimony.

[3] Luehrmann, *Religion in Secular Archives*, 75.

[4] Cristina Vățulescu. *Police Aesthetics: Literature, Film and the Secret Police in Soviet Times* (Stanford University Press, 2010).

The Hidden Galleries Digital Archive

The images and stories presented in this book have been selected from the Hidden Galleries Digital Archive (http://hiddengalleries.eu/digitalarchive/), which presents more detailed analyses of these and many other materials. Each story in this book corresponds to one or more digital archive entries, references to which can be found at the end of each text.

The rationale behind the digital archive, and by extension the public exhibitions and this volume which grew out of it, is to present visual and textual materials relating to the creative practices and material culture of the religious underground within the archives of the secret police. These materials have in many cases not been preserved elsewhere and are also difficult to access and locate within the secret police archives. The collection is indicative rather than comprehensive, with examples selected for the collection designed to demonstrate the kinds of materials produced by and about the religious underground. It is hoped that the digital archive will be used by researchers, the public and, most importantly, by members of the communities that were targeted by the secret police.

---oOo---

PART I.
THE UNDERGROUND

UNDERGROUND SPACES

The term "religious underground," so often used by both the secret police and dissident religious groups during communism, had both a metaphorical and a literal meaning. Some groups that were refused legal status built or occupied alternative places of worship above ground but these were easily discovered and closed down or destroyed. Other clandestine and illegal religious groups opted to conduct their services and meetings or to hide their members and possessions in underground spaces. This was not a phenomenon solely of the communist era, however; in the history of Christianity many groups, especially monastic communities, have chosen to worship and live in subterranean spaces. In Orthodox Christianity there are many examples of sacred underground complexes that could serve as a model for the creation of new underground places of worship when circumstances required it. Many different groups used underground spaces during the course of the twentieth century and examples can be found in Ukraine, Romania, Moldova and Hungary amongst both Orthodox dissent movements and so-called sects of Protestant or Evangelical origin, such as Adventists or Jehovah's Witnesses.

Underground places of worship were often dug specifically for the purpose, although existing cellars and caves were also sometimes used. These underground spaces varied in size, complexity and artistry, from small priesthole-type hiding places to vast underground complexes. They were dug in both rural and urban settings, but were more easily realized and concealed in the countryside. Religious gatherings conducted in subterranean spaces might demand certain changes such as the modification of the spatial and material aspects of ritual or the reduction in the number of those present at certain gatherings.

Typically, the images we find in the secret police archives were taken as crime scene photographs and as such they were concerned with showing the means of concealment of entrances to underground spaces, the route of entry and actual hidden space. In some cases, the secret police also captured in photographs and films the enforced re-enactment of ritual in these spaces.

Source
Source © National Council for the Study of the Securitate Archives (ConsiliulNaţional pentru Studierea Arhivelor Securităţi -CNSAS), I161963, vol. 1.

1.
Destruction of a Romanian Old Calendarist Church
-
Iuliana Cindrea

These photographs were taken in 1935, in the village of Cucova, in the county of Putna (today's Bacău county), as evidence of the so-called rebellion launched by the Old Calendarists in the region. The events at Cucova were part of a general religious dissent movement that began when many Orthodox believers refused to accept the introduction of the solar aspect of the Revised Julian calendar in the Romanian Orthodox Church in 1924.

The context in which these photographs were taken is very important for the history of the Old Calendarist Church. The incidents are described as a massacre in the narratives of the Old Calendarists, while the archival documents portray the event in a different light, making the Old Calendarists appear as rebels and troublemakers. Even though it is not very clear what caused the incident, the fact that Cucova had become a gathering place for Old Calendarists from different regions might have been a reason for the authorities' intervention. Police reports state that the Old Calendarist believers hid in their improvised church and soon became violent, forcing the gendarmerie to use firearms. Based on some archival documents and other sources, five people were killed, 28 wounded and 40 arrested (the places where two of them were shot are marked with red crosses in one of the photographs).

These images, taken after the gendarmes captured the church, give us important information about the operation and its aftermath. The number of women depicted in one photograph supports the contemporary view that women played an important role in the Old Calendarist communities (see entry 8). The same assertion is supported by both secret police reports and numerous newspaper articles that accuse Old Calendarist women of attempting to lure and trick people into becoming members of the community.

The wooden church itself, which was surrounded by a wooden fence, is pictured with window frames removed. This could indicate the intention of the authorities to completely destroy it but keep any valuable building materials. According to the narratives of the Old Calendarists, the church was destroyed soon after this event. The photo of the interior of the church is of great value as it allows us to see how objects and icons were originally displayed. It was taken from the inside of the church and captures the intrusive gaze of three gendarmes (shown in the centre of the photo) into the sacred space. Large icons appear to have been removed from the wall but there are numerous small icons still in place.

In 1936, one year after this event, police reports state that the Old Calendarist movement was no longer active in the region. Even though the wooden church in Cucova was destroyed in 1935, an Old Calendarist monastery, which still stands today, was later rebuilt on approximately the same site.

Source

Digital Archive entry
http://hiddengalleries.eu/digitalarchive/s/en/item/3

161
1
2
3

2.
True Orthodox Underground Monastery
-
Tatiana Vagramenko

After the Bolshevik Revolution in 1917, political repression first turned against the Russian Orthodox Church. The majority of monasteries and churches were closed down and many former priests, nuns and monks continued their religious practices underground, in private houses and apartments, often wandering from village to village. Various catacomb Orthodox communities formed what became known as the True Orthodox movement.

In the 1940s, the Ukrainian secret police discovered a whole network of underground churches and monasteries in the Kharkiv region (Ukraine), led by the priest and monk Seraphim (Shevtsov) (see also entry 19). Between 1940 and 1960, the secret police destroyed over 15 such constructions. In 1945, the police raided one of the underground monasteries in the town of Chuhuiv. When the police broke into the monastery, they found some 20 people praying there. Most of them were monks and nuns who were living underground. Seraphim was amongst them.

These photographs were taken during the raid and are the only surviving visual record of the subterranean monastery, which was later destroyed by the police. The entrance to the monastery was concealed within the wall of a vault by a wooden structure. Inside, however, it looked impressive. Arched galleries led to many chambers: several bedrooms, a storage space with a stove and a mill, and finally to a subterranean church with its altar and iconostasis.

Records of Seraphim's interrogations give a detailed account of how underground churches and monasteries were constructed and how the religious life of communities of Orthodox dissenters was organized. Seraphim claimed that there were about 2,000 believers under his leadership from different parts of eastern Ukraine and southern Russia. The underground church could accommodate up to 300 people at a time with a core group of 10-15 monastics who lived there permanently under the spiritual guidance of father Seraphim.

Even in the religious underground, there was constant mobility. As more people came, the subterranean structure was expanded and modified. When a place was discovered or became unsafe, believers built new underground churches, moving from village to village. In the interrogation report, Seraphim explains about an incident that happened in the underground monastery in 1941. The subterranean structure partly collapsed when a group of believers gathered for prayer. The tragedy took the life of four people who were then secretly buried in the same underground church where they had died. Monks and nuns belonging to the community were also buried inside the underground church.

The police continued to arrest Seraphim's followers after his detention. In 1948, the MGB (as the Soviet secret police were known at the time) reported the arrest of a group of wandering monastics left uprooted after Seraphim's imprisonment and the closure of the underground monastery. Seraphim returned to his community after his release in 1952 and continued to build more underground churches. He was secretly buried in one of them in 1955.

Source

Digital Archive entry

http://hiddengalleries.eu/digitalarchive/s/en/item/144

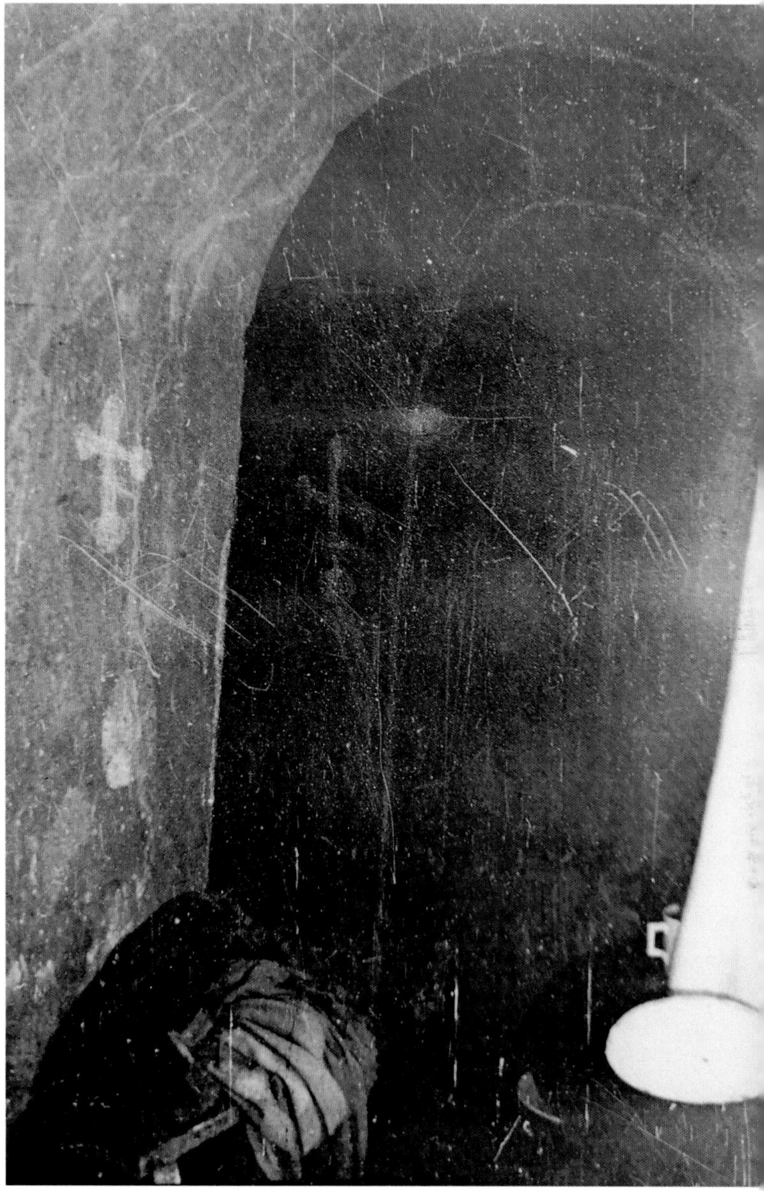

3.

Underground Monastery in Bucharest

\-

Anca Maria Șincan

Between 1965 and 1983, the Old Calendarist underground monastery in Bucharest was raided over and over again, but each time the community rebuilt it in defiance of the secret police. These photographs, which document a sweep operation that ended in the destruction of the underground church and the arrest of the leader of the bishop of the church, Evloghie Oța, cannot be dated precisely but appear in a secret police personal file and were used as evidence of the underground monastery (see also entries 10 and 52). According to the legal framework of the communist state, the Old Calendarist Orthodox Church was an illegal entity. Although the secret police implied that the community was hiding underground, the Old Calendarist subterranean religious space and underground chapels were not necessarily used for hiding in, but instead conform with the Orthodox Christian monastic tradition of locating sites of worship in caves and subterranean spaces.

The community was formed in 1964 when their bishop was released from prison. Over the 26 years of the community's existence their number gradually increased. There were several brothers who lived in the monastery as well as a parish that consisted of regular church-goers and people that travelled from time to time from various places across Romania. Bishop Oța would also sometimes visit distant members of his flock and correspond with them via letters. This form of parish, which was not typical for a regular Romanian Orthodox Church, enabled the Old Calendarist community to survive the repressive policies of the communist regime.

The secret police file from which these images originate contains several other photographs as well as maps of the house and the underground chapel. Following standard crime scene photographic principles, the array of images illustrate the exterior and the means of entry to the underground chapel as well as the main incriminating evidence and close up details of particular elements that elucidate the crime. The pictures we see here illustrate common tropes of illegal religious activity: the secret entrance to the underground and the ritual space itself is shown as well as believers seemingly caught in the act of worship.

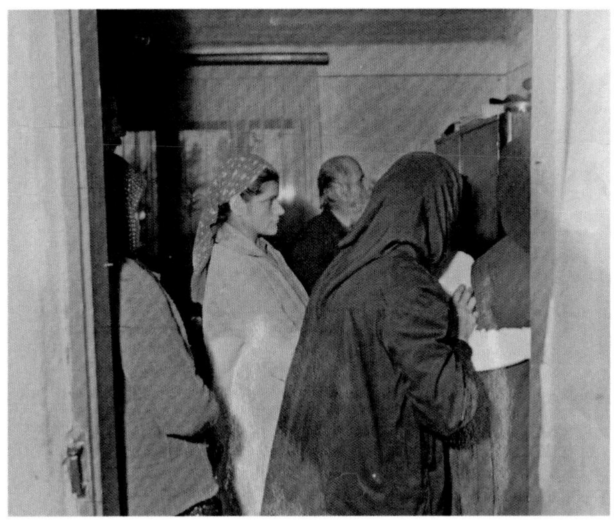

Source

Digital Archive entry

http://hiddengalleries.eu/digitalarchive/s/en/item/24

4.
Bunker Printing Press
-
Tatiana Vagramenko

In 1955, the police raided an underground bunker printing press operated by Jehovah's Witnesses in a rural location in western Ukraine. The photographs taken during the raid were pasted into a fourteen-volume criminal file against seven Jehovah's Witness leaders.

The bunker was constructed under a rural private house in Smodne village that was also used as a safe house where several members of the Jehovah's Witness organization hid to avoid arrest. The photographs show a bunker airway masked with sheaves, an entrance box from the bunker, as well as confiscated printing equipment (rotator, wax stencil, paper, typeface and ink) and samizdat religious materials discovered in the bunker. One of the photographs depicts an arrested believer (and the owner of the house) sitting with the confiscated items.

The bunker printing press was discovered by the police in 1955 as a result of a major secret operation against the Witness leadership in Ukraine. Among the arrested persons was Bohdan Terletsky, the leader of the Jehovah's Witnesses in the Soviet Union from 1953 to 1955, who had been on a secret police wanted list since 1950. Under intense pressure and after numerous interrogations, Terletsky's spirit was broken and he agreed to cooperate with the secret police. Later, during the 1960s, he would give evidence at trials against other Jehovah's Witnesses.

The Soviet authorities considered the Witnesses an anti-Soviet organization and denied them legal recognition. They became one of the largest categories of political prisoners in the whole socialist bloc. Being outlawed, Jehovah's Witnesses were kept under close surveillance and were subjected to intense harassment including home raids, confiscation of Bibles and religious literature, mass arrests and show trials with subsequent long-term imprisonment and detention in labour camps. The Soviet authorities initiated two major deportations of the Witnesses and their families from the western Ukrainian borderland, Moldova, Belarus, Latvia, Lithuania and Estonia (in 1949 and 1951). As a result, over 10,000 Witnesses and their families (including children and elderly) were exiled to "special settlements" in Siberia and Transbaikal.

Jehovah's Witnesses in the Soviet Union ran one of the most active and complex underground networks with internal hierarchy and leadership, a coded reporting system and finances, networks of printing presses, smuggling operations and clandestine communication channels. Despite mass repression, the Witnesses proved remarkably resilient with the number of members steadily growing.

Source

Digital Archive entry

http://hiddengalleries.eu/digitalarchive/s/en/item/188

5. Raid on a House Church

–

Kinga Povedák

These pictures have been selected from a set of 27 crime scene photographs that were taken during a raid on pastor József Németh's Pentecostal community in a hidden house church in Budapest (see also entry 44). The raid took place on 26 September 1972 during a regular Tuesday gathering.

Németh's community had been under surveillance since 1968 when he separated from the Evangelical Christian Church (Evangéliumi Keresztény Egyház), which was the officially recognized Pentecostal organization, after being accused of a series of misdemeanours by the Church. Following this, the secret police initiated an investigation on the grounds that the religious group held no official permit to operate. In 1972 the secret police decided to take action and according to the investigation file the following objectives were set out: a) end the illegal religious activity; b) collect evidence for the illegal activity; and c) assess the valuables of the illegal community. The main accusation against József Németh and his congregation was the misuse of the right to freedom of association. The secret police used an anonymous note written by a citizen as a pretext (a common practice of the Hungarian secret police) in order to justify a raid on the community. After the house search, József Németh and other leading figures in the community were interrogated on several occasions. Pastor József Németh received a suspended sentence of three months.

The photographs taken during the raid depict the hidden church in József Németh's house in Pesterzsébet. We see congregants, some of whom are facing the table-altar discussing the unfolding situation whilst others are turning towards the back of the room in order to follow events. Behind the altar, the double doors are covered with curtains, which frame the altar. Another image depicts the back of the room with congregants and possibly two secret police officers seated against the back wall. Amongst the objects found in the raid, an electric organ was considered suspect and evidence of illegal economic activity.

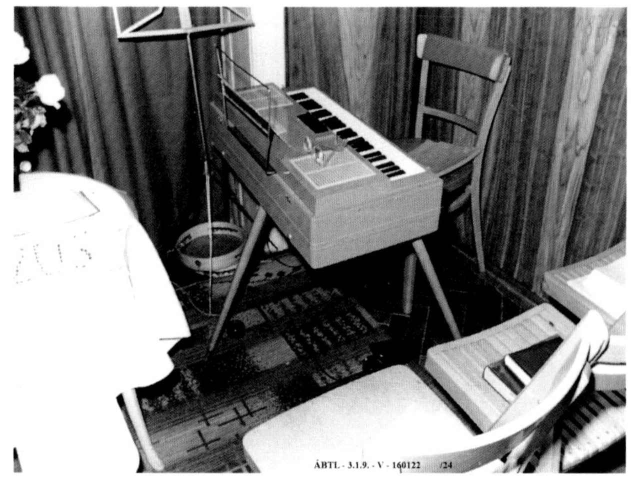

Source

Digital Archive entry

http://hiddengalleries.eu/digitalarchive/s/en/item/6

JÉZUS

6. Renouncing Membership of the Romanian Orthodox Church

–

Anca Maria Șincan

In the spring of 1973 a series of almost identical handwritten, signed and dated letters were sent to the Romanian Orthodox parish in Lugoj. The authors inform the Orthodox Church in Lugoj that they are leaving the Church. One of the letters, written in the name of an entire family, states that if as children they had been mistakenly registered with the Orthodox Church they now respectfully ask to be removed from the church records and with this act they declare themselves to be Roman Catholic believers.

According to the explanation given to the Ministry for Religious Denominations by the local Orthodox archbishop, the authors of the letters were former Greek Catholic believers who had joined the Orthodox Church in 1948. The archbishop's communication goes on to identify the authors as older and helpless members of the former Greek Catholic Church, one of whom was a bedridden former Greek Catholic priest. These letters, which were required according to the Law on the General State of Religious Denominations that outlines the official process of leaving one denomination and joining another, were part of a larger campaign by the underground Greek Catholic Church aimed at the legalization of their Church. Such letters demonstrate that the Greek Catholic community was still very much active in the 1970s and that its members were openly leaving the Orthodox Church in protest at the 1948 forced unification. The letters also show that after the forceful unification between the Orthodox Church and the Greek Catholic Church, in some cases believers were registered as Orthodox without their knowledge or agreement.

These letters were forwarded to the secret police by the Ministry for Religious Denominations, where they were received together with the Orthodox archbishop's letter requesting the ministry's help in discovering who instigated this action and seeking solutions to the problems it raised. The matter was investigated by the secret police and deemed not dangerous, with the officers leading the investigation reporting that the authors of the letters were old and the sole reason they had drafted them was so they could prepare for their death. The Roman Catholic Church could not or would not officiate at the funerals of registered Orthodox believers and thus the authors of the letters had to officially leave the Orthodox Church even if, at least in some cases, they had never officially joined it.

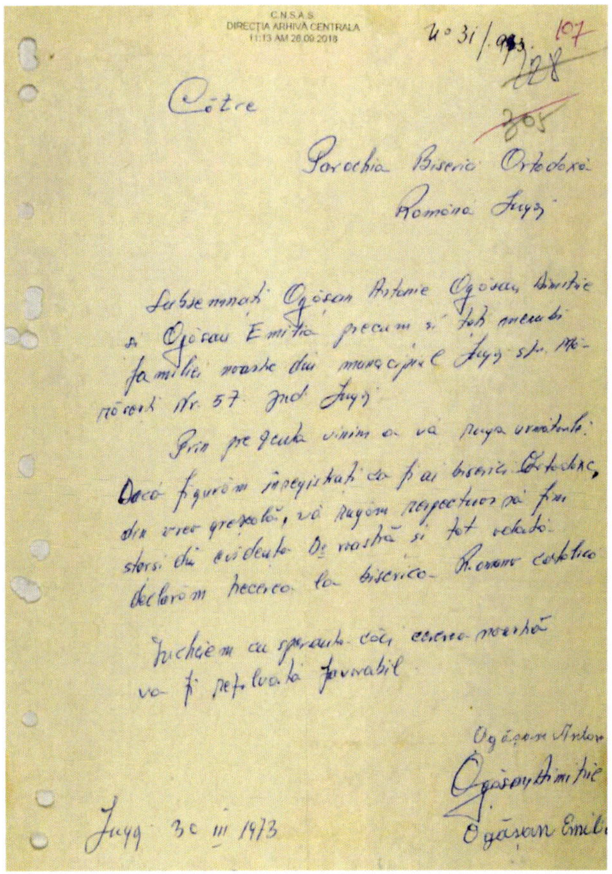

CNSAS
DIRECȚIA ARHIVĂ CENTRALA
11:13 AM 28.09.2018

Nr. 31/1973

Către

Parohia Bisericii Ortodoxe Române Lugoj

Subsemnații Ogășan Antonie, Ogășan Dimitrie și Ogășan Emilia precum și toți membrii familiei noastre din municipiul Lugoj str. Mărăști Nr. 57 jud. Lugoj

Prin prezenta venim a vă ruga următoarele:

Dacă figurăm înregistrați ca fii ai bisericii Ortodoxe, din vreo greșeală, vă rugăm respectuos să fim șterși din evidența D-voastră și tot odată declarăm trecerea la biserica Romano catolica

Încheiem cu speranța că cererea noastră va fi rezolvată favorabil

Lugoj 30 III 1973

Ogășan Antonie
Ogășan Dimitrie
Ogășan Emilia

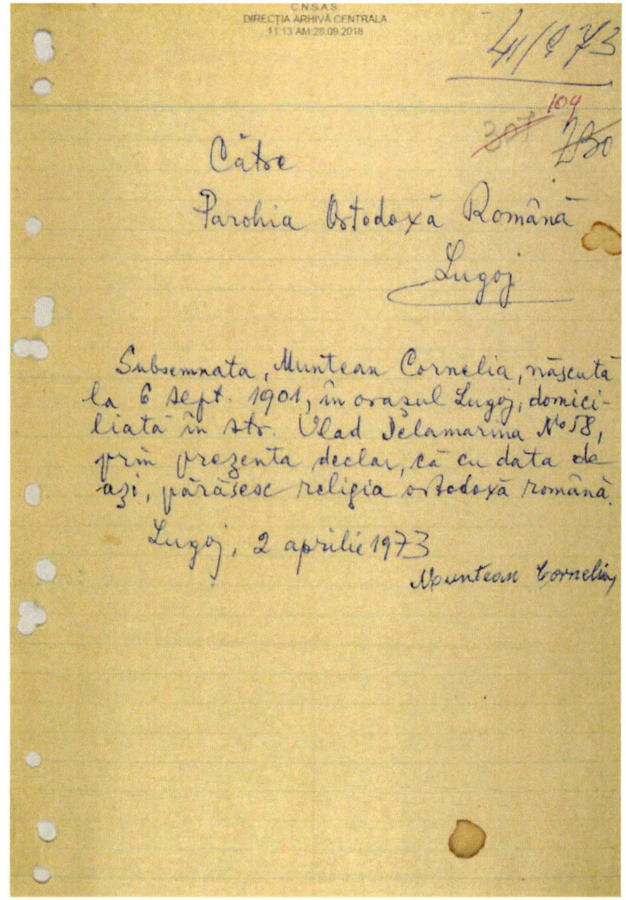

CNSAS
DIRECȚIA ARHIVĂ CENTRALA
11:13 AM 28.09.2018

41/1973

Către

Parohia Ortodoxă Română

Lugoj

Subsemnata, Muntean Cornelia, născută la 6 sept. 1901, în orașul Lugoj, domiciliată în str. Vlad Țelamarina No 58, prin prezenta declar, că cu data de azi, părăsesc religia ortodoxă română.

Lugoj, 2 aprilie 1973

Muntean Cornelia

Source

© National Council for the Study of the Securitate Archives (Consiliul Național pentru Studierea Arhivelor Securității-CNSAS), D69, vol. 9.

Digital Archive entry

http://hiddengalleries.eu/digitalarchive/s/en/item/307

7. Clandestine Greek Catholic Services in Transylvania

Anca Maria Șincan

These photographs of Greek Catholic religious life in 1970s Transylvania captured on camera by the community themselves represent a rare instance where it has been possible to relate secret police descriptions of religious life to photographic materials that can still be found in the community. The photographic images come from the private photo collection of Mihai and Ana Rus from Băița village, Mureș county, and were shown to the author during ethnographic fieldwork in August 2018. The family photo collection contains several images that are described in the secret police files on Bishop Alexandru Todea (see also entry 27). The Rus family could not pinpoint the date when they received the photos nor when they were taken; however, on 23 January 1971 the Securitate reported on the situation of the clandestine Greek Catholic community in Reghin, where Todea lived, and outlined the planned measures to be taken against the Greek Catholic community in the area that had been meeting at Bishop Todea's house. At the bottom of the page of the Securitate report it states that Bishop Alexandru Todea (secret police code name Toma Aurel) performed religious services all over the town as well as in his house, where he also conducted marriage services.

The Rus family's collection includes images of the very religious services reported by the secret police, including the couple's own wedding and the baptism and confirmation of their children. One of the photographs included here shows a well-attended liturgy in Bishop Todea's house led by an unidentified priest dressed in Roman Catholic liturgical vestments holding the chalice and a Greek Catholic priest (probably Father Augustin Giurgiu) holding the disk (ceremonial plate) with the unconsecrated Holy Body of Christ (the prosphora). This image shows that in this particular Byzantine service, the Roman Catholic priest holding the chalice was leading the liturgy.

The image of Bishop Alexandru Todea with his hands together in prayer was taken after his release from prison in 1964. It was probably taken at his request and served as a reminder for the underground community that he was alive and still performing his pastoral duties and that his church, which had been dismembered by the communist regime in 1948, was still functioning. Descriptions of similar photographic devotional materials appear in Todea's Securitate Informative file. Secret police agents and informers talk about a distribution network of pictures of Alexandru Todea and also mention that they were sold for three lei.

Source

Digital Archive entry

http://hiddengalleries.eu/digitalarchive/s/en/item/296

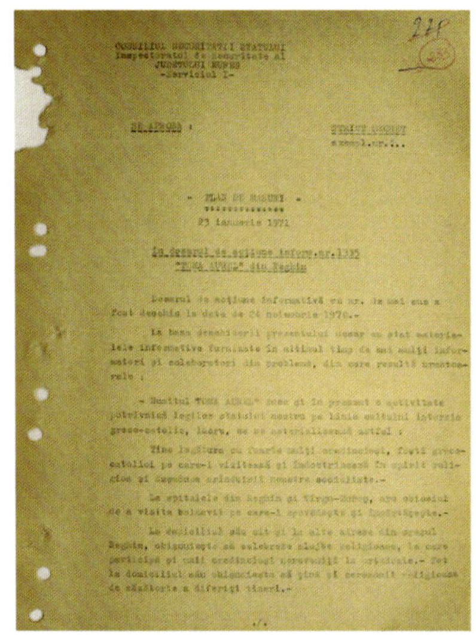

23 ianuarie 1971

8.
Nuns Hiding in the Woods
-
Iuliana Cindrea

In 1941 two Old Calendarist nuns, Steliana Geangu and Anica Măzărel, were discovered hiding in a hut in the Pralea Woods in Bacău county in Romania. A photograph, seemingly taken in a photography studio, was confiscated from one of them by the siguranța (the Romanian secret police prior to Communism). It depicts four Old Calendarist nuns. A short handwritten text on the reverse states that it was taken on 1 September 1939 and suggests that it was used as a personal memento: "Memory, this photo is mine, Singlitichia, developed on 1 September 1939. Here are M. Chiriachia, M. Melania and Sara Iliana and M. Singlitichia the Sinner."

Arrested and tried for "Stilist propaganda," the two nuns were accused of posing a danger to the interests of the state. State security archival sources report that the "Stilist phenomenon," as followers of the old style Calendar were sometimes called, had faded by 1940 and, indeed, leading up to 1936 the most important leaders of the group had been arrested. However, the community continued to exist underground. Some of them, referred to by the authorities as "vagabond priests and nuns," began meeting in attics, cellars or other secluded places, while others fled into the woods where they hid in caves and huts, like Steliana and Anica.

Amongst the documents that were also confiscated from them we find books and personal correspondence, but also confessions of believers, written down and sent to these two nuns, indicating that Steliana and Anica had become the confessors of some members of the community, a stance and duty that was usually associated with men. In the absence of a male figure, they even conducted church services by themselves in their small hut in the woods. They ensured their survival by knitting gloves and socks and exchanging them for food. After 1941 I could find no trace of Steliana or Anica in the archives, and neither could I discover anything about their lives prior to their arrest.

Later, while going through the letters and postcards that Old Calendarist nuns who had been detained at Vărzărești Monastery sent to their families (entry 14), I came across a name that rang a bell. It was July 1937 when Dumitru Geangu, an Old Calendarist believer from Stănești, Tutova, declared that as the elder brother of Catinca, known as mother Chiriachia, who was being detained at Vărzărești, he felt the responsibility to send clothes and food to his sister. There is no postcard and no other mention of her name, except this short reminder that she was also one of the imprisoned nuns. Born in 1913, Catinca was detained at Vărzărești for taking part in the events that happened at Cucova in 1935, which resulted in the destruction of the Old Calendarist church in the village (see entry 1). Probably released by September 1939 (the date written on the back of the confiscated photo) Catinca, also known as Steliana, found shelter in the hut in the Pralea Woods together with Măzărel Anica.

The story of the nuns did not end with the last page of a penal file. During fieldwork in June 2019, while peering closely at my laptop in order to see the content of the penal file I had just opened, an Old Calendarist believer I was interviewing said, "Geangu is still a known name in our community." Then, while turning his head away from it, he fearfully asked, "what is this?" "These are some confessions that people would send to them," I naively replied, trying to make sense of what was happening. "These are personal, I don't want to see them, no one should read them," he said, while I was staring at him with a baffled look, counting in my mind the hours I had spent trying to decipher them. That was the first time I felt like an intruder, but I also realized how careless and intrusive the secret police were. "They are still part of the community, Geangu, maybe they will be happy to see the file, if you find a way to get it to them," his voice echoed, while I was still gathering my thoughts. I did find a way to get it to them and today, on 17 December 2019, as I am writing these lines, I look forward to hearing a better ending of the story.

Source

Digital Archive entry

http://hiddengalleries.eu/digitalarchive/s/en/item/2

9.
Maria Sîrbu and Her Sisters in Faith
-
James Kapaló

On 25 August 1938 a house search was conducted of the home of Vladimir Draguțan in the village of Recea, county Lăpușna in Bessarabia (today's Republic of Moldova), which was then under Romanian rule. Maria Sârbu, pictured here, was arrested together with Vladimir and his father Vasile and they were all found guilty of conducting Inochentist propaganda. Inochentism is the name given to a religious movement founded by an Orthodox monk, Inochentie (Innocent) that emerged in the border regions between Romania and Russia in the first decade of the twentieth century. They were found in possession of materials that seemed to show that they were active members of the Archangelist branch of the movement (see entries 23, 35 and 38). Maria Sîrbu confessed in her statement that she had "left her home village ten years previously and had been wandering as a vagabond with Inochentist sectants" ever since. During this period, women in particular are frequently reported as living as travelling preachers or propagandists for the movement, something that the Romanian gendarmerie and secret police struggled to put a stop to.

Amongst the evidence gathered at Vladimir's home were a number of items "used for Inochentist propaganda," including some religious booklets, a number of small crosses and several photographs of the community and their leaders. In this photograph of Maria Sârbu (who is probably the woman seated in the centre in the place of honour, although this is not stated in the file) and two of her sisters in the community, we can see that they wear silver crosses very prominently outside their clothing on long chains. Vladimir Drăguțan, in whose home Maria Sîrbu was arrested, was found to be making such "small crosses from silver, with all the kit necessary for making crosses." The gendarmes confiscated "three silver coins and five small crosses" and in his statement Vladimir admits to manufacturing them since 1931. The gendarme captain interprets the manufacture of crosses as a means to "cheat believers and sectants and with the sale of the crosses attract them from the Orthodox religion to the Inochentist sect."

In the absence of Inochentist written testimonies from this period, the materials found in the military court files present us with an important record of their material cultural practices. We can look upon Maria Sîrbu represented in the way she chose to be seen with her sisters in faith standing behind her both holding wooden crosses in their right hands—the symbol of a martyr in Orthodox iconography and a direct infringement of Orthodox canonical norms regarding visual representations of people who are not saints.

Source

© National Archives of the Republic of Moldova (Arhiva Națională a Republicii Moldova-ANRM), fond Tribunalul militar al Corpului III armată, dosar. 738-1-6846.

Digital Archive entry

http://hiddengalleries.eu/digitalarchive/s/en/item/85

10.

Floorplan of an Underground House Church

-

Anca Maria Șincan

Bishop Evloghie Oța of the Old Calendarist Orthodox Church (see entry 3) was released from prison in 1964 in the general amnesty decree. Soon after, he re-established his community and built his church in Televiziunii Street in Bucharest. The secret police lost no time in opening an individual file and starting a surveillance operation.

The two images show house floorplans that were drawn by the police during their surveillance operation. Two handwritten documents precede the two drawings of the house layout. They are from two successive years and originate from the local policemen (called *sectorist* in Romanian) that supervised the area where Bishop Evloghie Oța built his house church. The first document from December 1964 represents the first meeting of the local policeman with the new neighbours, whom he describes as "people dressed in monastic uniforms." The second, following soon after, was a more detailed account by a lieutenant who entered the house to ask for the house documents and encountered four persons, Bishop Evloghie among them, in a "prayer session, in possession of religious books, religious vestments and icons representing church figures." One can safely assume that the first house layout drawing (on the left) was created by this lieutenant. The document, in which he asked for further instructions, was sent to his superiors and ended up with the secret police to later be used during the first destruction of the Old Calendarist Orthodox Church in Televiziunii Street.

The house floorplan drawing is thorough. It has an explanatory legend and uses different colours to distinguish between important and less important areas. At number 4 on the legend we find the church room that is adjacent to the bishop's room. The plan also shows that a policeman lived in a house across the street from the underground house church.

Based on this initial layout, a slightly different plan was made. The second house layout (on the right) acknowledges Bishop Oța's ownership of the house. It also shows the way, using blue arrows, to enter the house. This layout was used in the later secret police operation in 1965 when the church was destroyed and the bishop arrested again (see entry 3).

Source

© National Council for the Study of the Securitate Archives (Consiliul Național pentru Studierea Arhivelor Securității-CNSAS), fond Informativ, I 161963, vol. 1.

Digital Archive entry

http://hiddengalleries.eu/digitalarchive/s/en/item/389

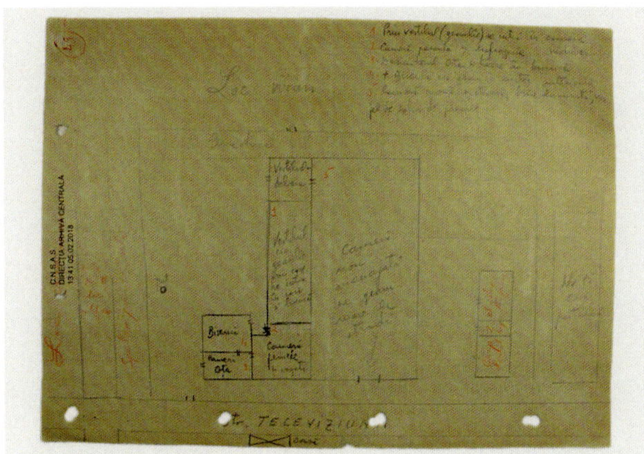

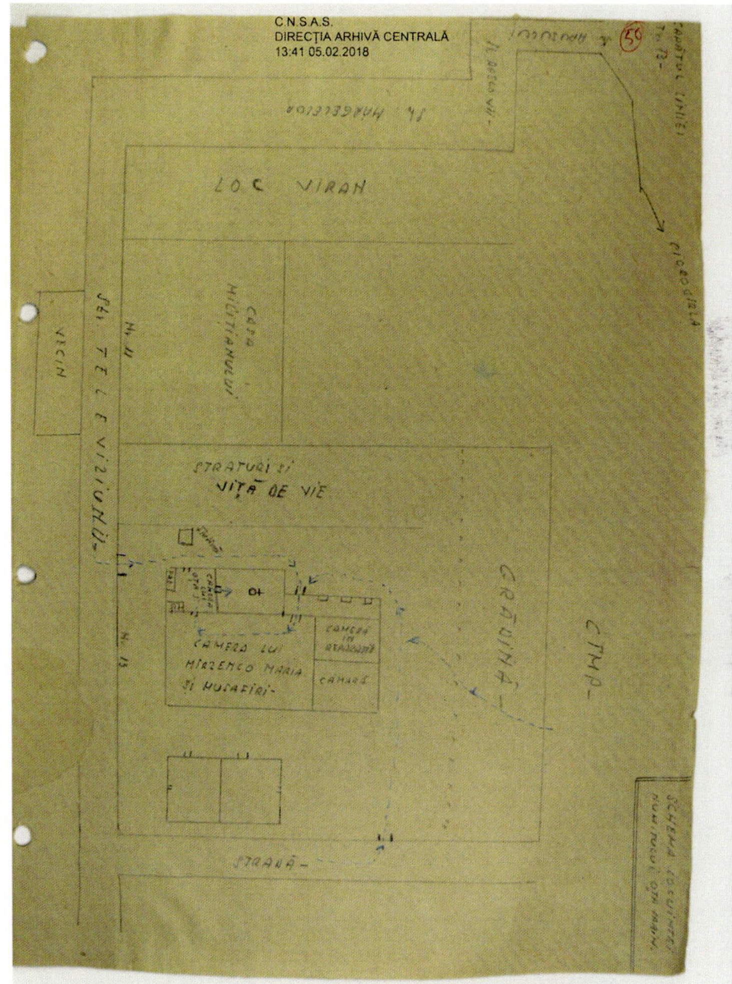

COMMUNICATING IN THE UNDERGROUND

A key to the survival of underground religious groups was the ability to communicate with one another without being discovered by the authorities. To this end, communities developed various communication strategies. Some, like the heavily persecuted Jehovah's Witnesses, communicated in coded reports, operated a complex system of trusted couriers to deliver messages and religious materials and used cover names for their leaders. It was common practice amongst clandestine religious groups to rely heavily on orally transmitted messages and to use coded language, ambiguous wording and omissions in both oral and written communication. Also, part of the communication strategy of some groups was to limit the amount of information known to each individual member, thus protecting the wider network.

The secret police made considerable efforts to map communication networks within the religious underground and to intercept transmitted messages, as they were often of key importance in unravelling and controlling clandestine religious activities. Examples of these kinds of communication methods and techniques are abundant in secret police files. They are usually presented as evidence of the hostile and conspiratorial nature of religious communities because of both the content of their messages and the secretive nature of their communication practices.

11.
Clandestine Catechism Classes
-
Ágnes Hesz

This handwritten letter was sent from Budapest in September 1954 recommending a catechism teacher who would give clandestine classes to children. Photocopies of the letter and the envelope were included in a documentary file on underground Roman Catholic religious groups that were connected to a movement lead by György Bulányi, a piarist monk. Though the letter only mentions the surname of the catechism teacher, Barlai, he is most probably identical with Ödön Szabolcs Barlay, a former Cistercian monk and teacher, who is featured in many other Hungarian secret police files. He was imprisoned in 1958 and again in 1961 for organizing illegal religious youth groups and giving illegal catechism classes.

In the letter, which is written on a piece of graph paper, the author provides precise information about when and where to contact this person. It also contains instructions on how to get to the location of the meeting, a private flat. The visit of the person addressed in the letter, a doctor's wife who was looking for a religious teacher for her daughters, was already expected by the catechism teacher, who had been notified of her intentioned visit. Near the end of the short and rather straightforward text, the writer, a widow, notes: "This has to be kept secret, obviously."

Although there is no additional information in the file about the identities of the corresponding partners, the letter gives some clues about their relationship and social background. The writer uses a form of address, "My Honourable Lady," typical of the old regime, and notes at the very end of the letter that "the clothes are ready." This suggests that she may have been a seamstress or a laundress and the addressee was one of her clients. It is also apparent from the letter that the sender knew the catechism teacher and wrote of him with the greatest respect, describing him as an extraordinary person and a superb speaker whose sermons were attended by "thousands."

The letter was written four years after the Hungarian government made the previously compulsory catechism classes optional in schools. Although it remained technically possible to receive religious education, parents were strongly discouraged from enrolling their children in these classes. As a 1955 informer report from another file reveals, even catechism teachers in schools were instructed to try to reduce the number of students in their classes. For those wanting to learn about religion, private catechism classes held by one of the several clandestine religious organizations and movements were often the only option. The authority deemed these classes illegal and pursued their teachers, who were priests, former monks and nuns or lay activists. Getting involved in these classes in any way was risky, and as this letter illustrates, finding a teacher or accepting a student was a matter of trust, in which people relied on their personal relations.

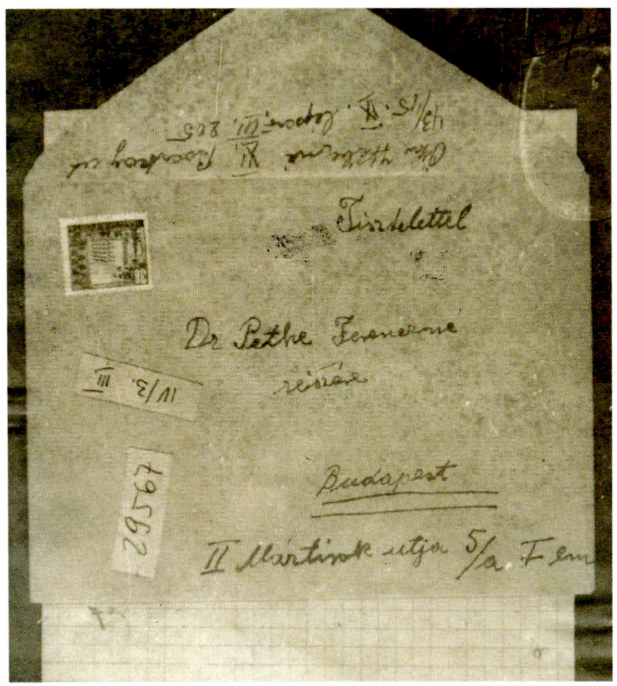

Source

Digital Archive entry
http://hiddengalleries.eu/digitalarchive/s/en/item/21

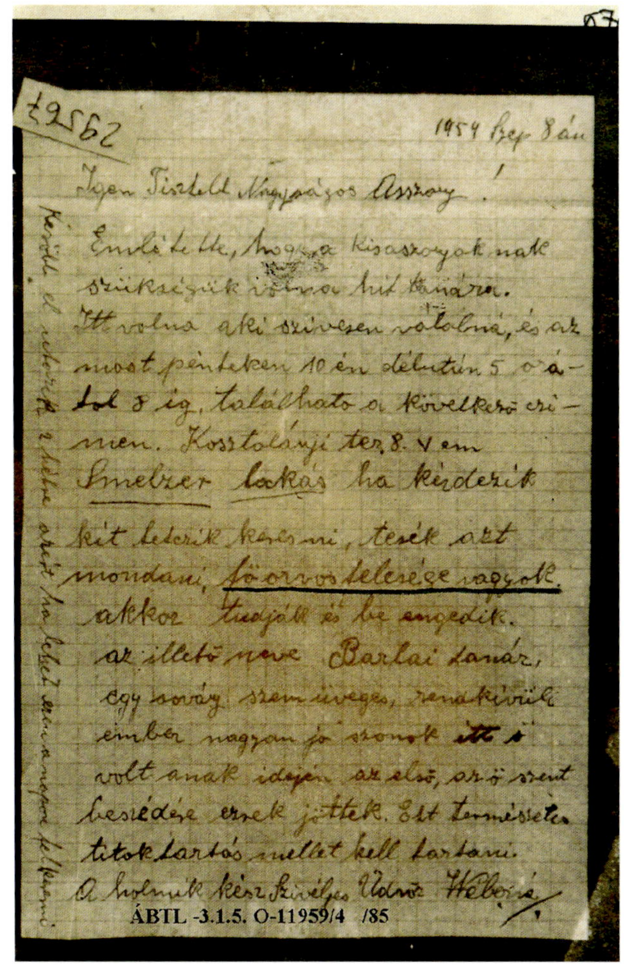
29562
1954 Szep. 8án
Igen Tisztelt Nagyságos Asszony!
Említette, hogy a kisasszonyoknak szükségük volna hittanárra. Itt volna aki szívesen vállalná, és az most pénteken 10én délután 5 órától 8ig található a következő címen. Kosztolányi tér 8. V em. Smelzer lakás ha kiderít kit keresni, tessék azt mondani, főorvos [illegible] akkor tudják és be engedik. az illető neve Barlai tanár, egy sovány szemüveges, rendkívüli ember nagyon jó szónok [illegible] volt [illegible] idején az első, az ő szent beszédére ezrek jöttek. Ezt természetes titoktartás mellett kell tartani. A holmik kész Szívélyes Üdvöz [illegible]
ÁBTL -3.1.5. O-11959/4 /85

12.
"Fresh Bread from Mama": Jehovah's Witness Code
-
Tatiana Vagramenko

Being surveilled and under constant risk of arrest, many clandestine religious communities developed their own coded language to communicate with each other and with their religious centres. This enabled them to avoid the disclosure of sensitive information in case of arrest and confiscation.

Jehovah's Witnesses were among the groups that had their own coded system of communication with special codes for use in their missionary materials and finance reports and tallies. The secret police, in turn, made great efforts to intercept clandestine communication channels and to decipher coded messages.

The missionary tallies shown here were confiscated by the Soviet KGB from a group of arrested Jehovah's Witnesses in western Ukraine. They report about the so-called "field service" of Witness western circuits in Ukraine during the period 1953-1954. The encrypted reports contain information about the number of believers in local groups, the amount of religious literature produced and distributed and hours spent evangelizing, as well as information about prayer meetings and Bible study groups, christenings and other religious events.

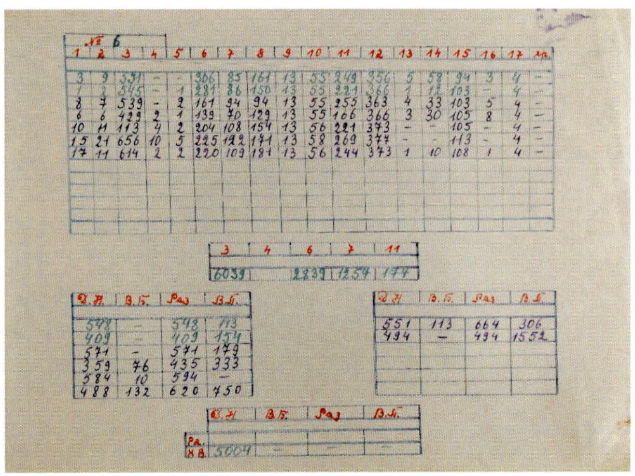

In their personal correspondence, Witnesses often described their religious experience using metaphors. For example, "fresh food" or "white bread" signified religious literature; "wine"—preaching God's Word; "Mamma"—the Watch Tower Society; "kolkhoz"—the faith community.

In 1952 the KGB intercepted a letter written by a Witness believer, which turned out to be a coded message about a religious gathering in his faith community:

Our family is healthy, we all are working in the kolkhoz and our work is going very well... We receive everything from our office. Once mamma baked white bread, and the wine was very tasty. It was brother Yuri who poured out the wine. The brigadier of the kolkhoz invited all the group leaders for the party and they were telling about the work in their units. As we were drinking wine, were getting merry and started singing then...

Source

© State Archive Branch of the Security Services of Ukraine (Haluzevyi derzhavnyi arkhiv Sluzhby bezpeky Ukrainy-HDA SBU), fond 5, spr. 42795, vol. 14.

Digital Archive Entry

http://hiddengalleries.eu/digitalarchive/s/en/item/378

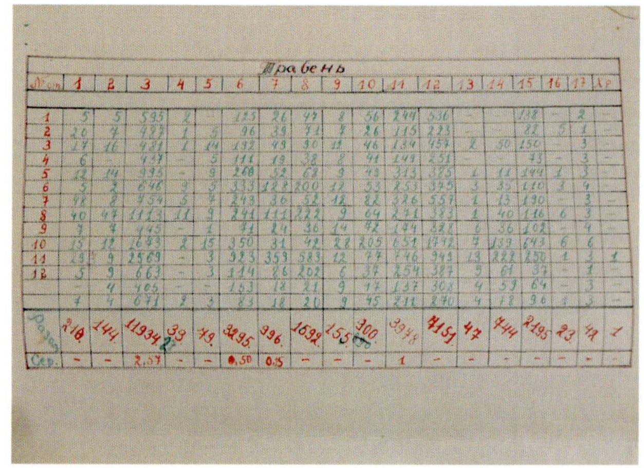

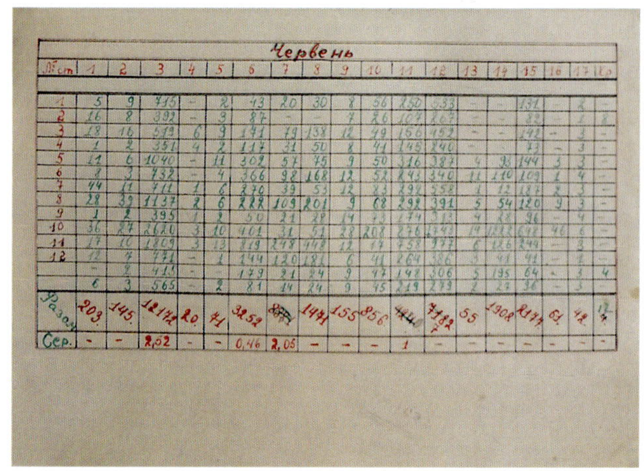

13.
"Catholic Girls"
-
Ágnes Hesz

This image comes from a documentary file, titled "Catholic Girls," on the former leaders of KLOSZ (National Confederation of Catholic Girls). KLOSZ was a Hungarian Catholic youth organization, founded in 1923 to provide extra-curricular education for girls and young women to help them become modern and active Catholic women. It lost its legal recognition in 1946 when nearly all civil organizations were dissolved by law. KLOSZ nevertheless continued its original work underground, with its leading figures and some of its members participating actively in underground Catholic movements.

The image shows an intercepted letter, an envelope and two holy cards. The message on the card is rather enigmatic:

I'm writing hastily, my dear Margit, asking Gizi not to write to our brother-in-law—on the contrary, if he happens to come here, she should tell him not to make any inquiries in this matter for now—and he should also return what he had noted down—I will explain if I visit you—Hugs, [illegible name].

According to a note made by the secret police in the file, the letter was posted on 27 May 1953. The header on the envelope originally displayed KLOSZ, but is has been taped over. Other than this, there is no information about the identity of the corresponding parties or the meaning and importance of the letter. However, the context and the other confiscated letters contained in the file suggest that it is an example of how clandestine religious communities communicated and organized their activities. Aware of being surveilled by the secret police, these groups were cautious in their actions and had various strategies to safely transmit information: they relied on oral communication whenever possible and used coded language or ambiguous wording if writing was unavoidable. In this case, for example, we may assume that the term "brother-in-law" stood for a cleric participating in the movement.

Source
© Historical Archives of the Hungarian State Security (Állambiztonsági Szolgálatok Történeti Levéltára-ÁBTL), 3.1.5 O-10202.
Digital Archive entry
http://hiddengalleries.eu/digitalarchive/s/en/item/340

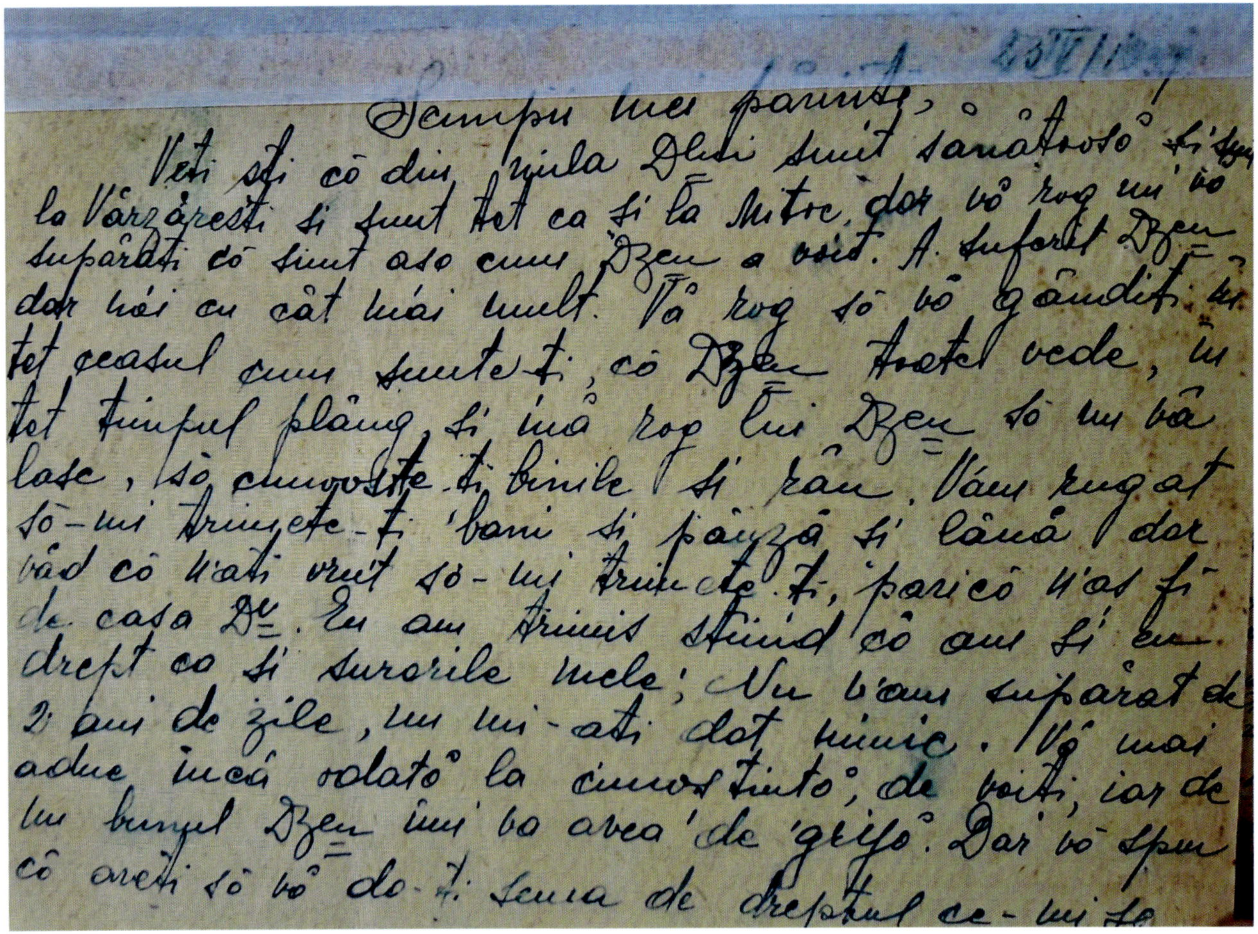

Scumpii mei părinţi,
Veţi şti că din mila D-lui sunt sănătoasă şi sunt
la Vărzăreşti şi sunt tot ca şi la Mitre, dar vă rog nu vă
supăraţi că sunt aşa cum D-zeu a voit. A suferit D-zeu
dar nici cu cât mai mult. Vă rog să vă gândiţi în
tot ceasul cum sunteţi, că D-zeu toate vede, în
tot timpul plâng şi mă rog lui D-zeu să nu vă
lase, să cunoaşteţi binele şi răul. V-am rugat
să-mi trimeteţi bani şi pânză şi lână dar
văd că n-aţi vrut să-mi trimeteţi, parcă n-aş fi
de casa D-v. Eu am trimis ştiind că am şi eu
drept ca şi surorile mele; Nu v-am supărat de
2 ani de zile, nu mi-aţi dat nimic. Vă mai
aduc încă odată la cunoştinţă, de voiţi, iar de
nu bunul D-zeu îmi va avea de grijă. Dar vă spun
că aveţi să vă daţi seama de dreptul ce-mi se

14.
Postcard from Detention
-
Iuliana Cindrea

This postcard was sent by an Old Calendarist nun to her family whilst in detention. It was sent from Vărzărești Monastery, one of the Orthodox monasteries where Old Calendarist nuns were detained and forced to accept the New Calendar. The postcard offers us a glimpse of the emotions and personal challenges faced by nuns and women who rejected the Orthodox Church calendar reform (see also entry 8).

The young woman appears to have been rejected by her parents, for reasons that are not clear from the information we have, and writes about her sufferings that she had endured for the last two years. From the message that she wrote to her parents, she appears to accuse them of having forgotten about her during these hardships and she reminds them that she is still their daughter and shares the same rights as her other sisters. The reason for her being treated like this by her parents are not described in the postcard, but she makes a statement that might hint at it: "I always cry and pray to God that He won't abandon you, that you will get to know the good and the bad." The statement could imply that her parents disagreed with her decision of becoming a nun or that they might have accepted the New Calendar, thus putting them at odds with her adherence to the Old Calendar. Although the archives do not preserve a reply to her postcard and we are not aware of her fate, she seems convinced that there is reason to her suffering for her faith. This is a recurrent theme in the letters and postcards written by Old Calendarist women in detention.

Source

Digital Archive entry

http://hiddengalleries.eu/digitalarchive/s/en/item/204

CARTA POSTALA

ROMANIA

Romania
50 BANI · TRIMITERI POSTALE
FONDUL AVIATIEI

3 LEI 3

Dsale Domnului
Neculai Secu
Com. Carpinistea
Jud. Buzău
Cătun Valea Hotarului

PART II.
POLICE AESTHETICS

RELIGIOUS NETWORK SCHEMES

The secret police produced so-called network schemes of the religious underground. This was a common way to visualize the connections that made up religious communities. Such network schemes represented these communities as centralized insurgent political organizations and visualized them as vertical networks constructed as hierarchical schemes where all links and dots came to a centre.

At the very bottom were pictured local cells—basic religious groups located in villages and small towns. A dot (triangle, circle or rectangle) showed the number of people in a community. Through couriers, basic cells were grouped and linked to form regional sets of cells. The regional centres were subordinated eventually to the top—either a capital administrative-political centre or a foreign (politically hostile) organization—hence, all groups were made to fit the same organizational logic, whether this reflected reality or not.

The schemes both produced knowledge of a giant conspiratorial network and at the same time helped to plan operations to break the envisioned social relations and to cut off the links within the network. Sometimes, the aim was not to fully destroy the network but to place it under control and to re-forge social links within the community in a way that it would be the secret police that would crown the pyramid of every social network.

The network schemes were carefully and precisely designed, with some of them printed using very advanced photo-printing technology for the time. Others, however, were mere hand-drawn sketches. They were normally inserted into official reports, manuals or other internal top-secret publications of the secret police and were used to show the results in progress of secret police operations against the targeted groups.

СХЕМА всесоюзной контр-революционной монархической организации церковников „Истинно-православная церковь", ликвидированной Секретно-Политическим Отделом О.Г.П.У.

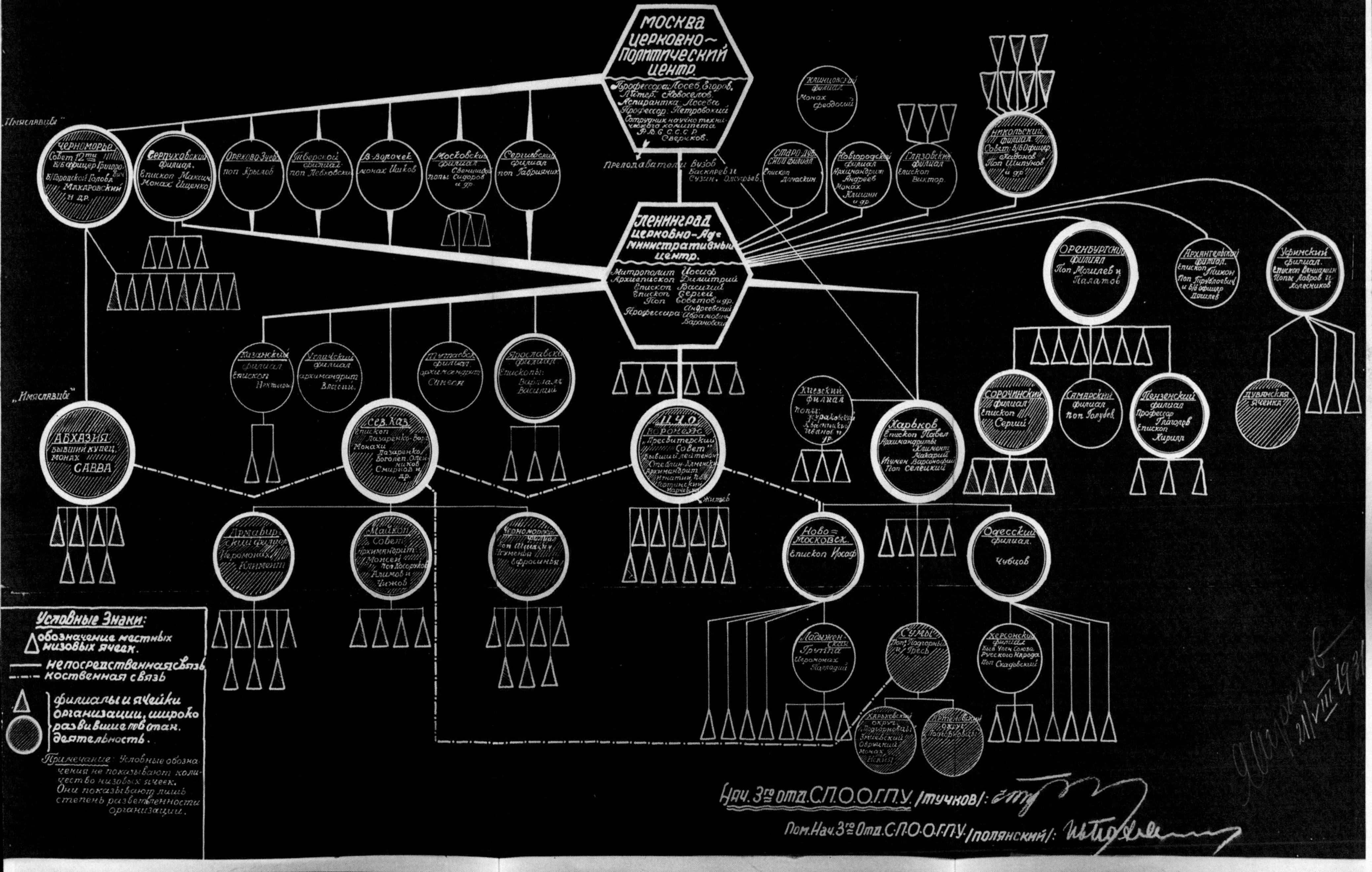

15.
Model Network Schemes
of the True Orthodox Church
-
Tatiana Vagramenko

The turbulent years of the Russian Revolution gave birth to numerous popular forms of Orthodox dissent that had an apocalyptic vision of a radically changing world, with Soviet power seen to be of the Antichrist or Satan. Numerous prophets and holy fools (*yurodivye*) preached the arrival of the Apocalyptic Red Dragon personified by the Communists. Hence, the Soviet secret police often used the phrase "red-dragon-type organization" when referring to these movements.

In 1930 Stalin's secret police (OGPU) launched the all-Union "liquidation campaign" against the growing Orthodox dissent movements, which they collectively referred to as the "ecclesiastical-monarchist underground." Among the repressed groups were numerous communities of the catacomb True Orthodox Church, which went under many names such as the Samosviatsy, Fedorovites, Ioannites and Stefanovites, and many other groups of ordinary believers.

These images (this page and previous page) come from two exemplary closing indictments against the catacomb True Orthodox Church. They were published in top secret brochures by the OGPU in 1931. The schemes picture communities of Orthodox dissenters dispersed in various regions of the Soviet Union as a counter-revolutionary organization with complex links and relations between cells and centres.

The scheme of the "All-Union counter-revolutionary monarchist ecclesiastic organization the True Orthodox Church" (previous page) is signed by Evgenii Tuchkov, the head of the so-called "Church Department" of the OGPU and one of the leaders of the anti-religious campaigns of the 1920s and 1930s. The scheme, which covers the entire Soviet Union, features shaded circles to refer to those cells and branches that had supposedly developed significant insurgent activities. The scheme gives two types of social connection: a direct link between the cells (solid lines) and an indirect link (dotted lines). It is unclear what an indirect link means here, but it allows for every group, branch and cell in the Soviet Union to be interconnected and at the same time subordinate to key regional centres and hierarchies.

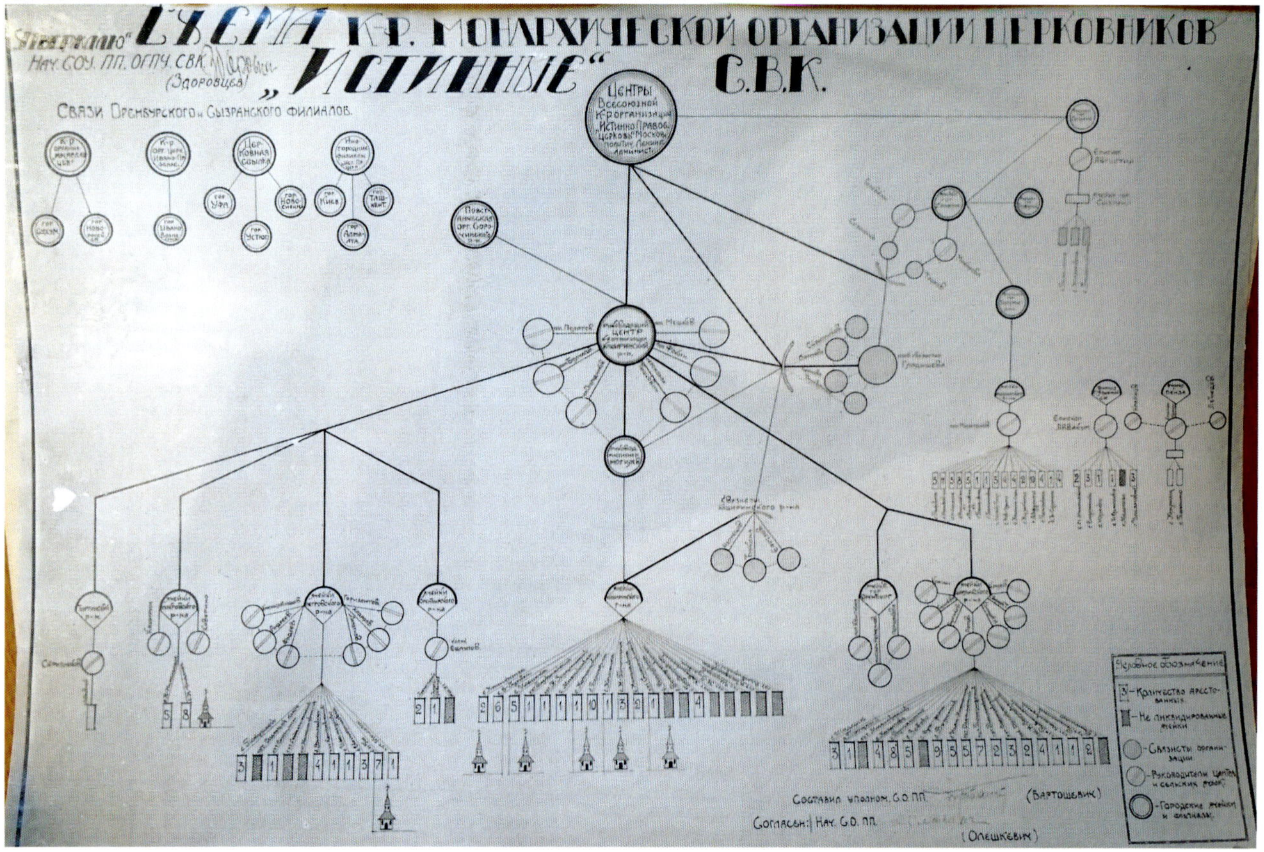

The network scheme from the Middle Volga region (above) shows miniature images of churches, which indicate basic cells centred around some churches that remain open. Circles twice crossed through refer to local leaders—a kulak, a priest, a monk, a bishop—or simply indicate surnames with no details. The links between cells are established through groups of couriers, schematically pictured as shaded circles. Through a similar group of couriers, the regional centre is connected eventually to the top. The all-union centres in Moscow and Leningrad crown both schemes. In this way, an ideal and comprehensive image of the insurgent, espionage, terrorist, counter-revolutionary, conspiratorial organization could be fully visualized.

Source
© State Archive Branch of the Security Services of Ukraine (Haluzevyi derzhavnyi arkhiv Sluzhby bezpeky Ukrainy-HDA SBU), fond 13, op. 1, spr. 386, 387.
Digital Archive entry
http://hiddengalleries.eu/digitalarchive/s/en/item/17

16.
Jehovah's Witness Network Scheme
-
Ágnes Hesz

In 1953 the Securitate started a so-called informative-operative operation against Jehovah's Witnesses in the former administrative region of Cluj, in Transylvania. Before 1990, with the exception of two short periods (1933–1937 and 1945–1949) Jehovah's Witnesses had no legal status in Romania and consequently suffered intense persecution at the hands of the inter-war democratic governments and the wartime dictatorship of Marshal Antonescu. The new operation against the Witnesses in Cluj started two years after the arrest and conviction of 35 members of the local leadership of the community. The aim of this wider operation was to identify the new leaders and functionaries of the reorganized regional units, to map their connections within and beyond the regional structure and to gather information about their activities and whereabouts. To further this goal, the Securitate employed several informants to infiltrate the group as well as relying on information gathered during interrogations of members arrested during the operation.

As part of this operation, a network scheme was produced and attached to an interim report written in 1955. The network scheme visualizes the results of the ongoing operation, showing the structure of Jehovah's Witnesses in Cluj region with names, ranks and connections of each of the functionaries (indicated by circles). The scheme aims to demonstrate that the Jehovah's Witnesses had a hierarchical structure. The blue box at the top stands for the national leaders, while the rectangular boxes at the bottom represent the six territorial units in the region with the number of their subunits and members. The scheme also informs the viewer of the progress the authorities had made in their measures against the group: arrested "elements" are indicated with red, while those still free are coloured with blue.

The basic units were the local congregations, each having its leader, called "servant." On a territorial basis, congregations formed circuits, with circuit servants responsible for coordinating the work of congregations. Communication between the levels was carried out with the help of couriers. Interaction within the group was highly secretive with most servants and evangelizers—called "pioneers"—having cover names for use even amongst other group members. All reports were coded, and couriers met with the leaders in crowded public places and used prearranged signs to get in touch with one another.

Source

Digital Archive entry
http://hiddengalleries.eu/digitalarchive/s/en/item/288

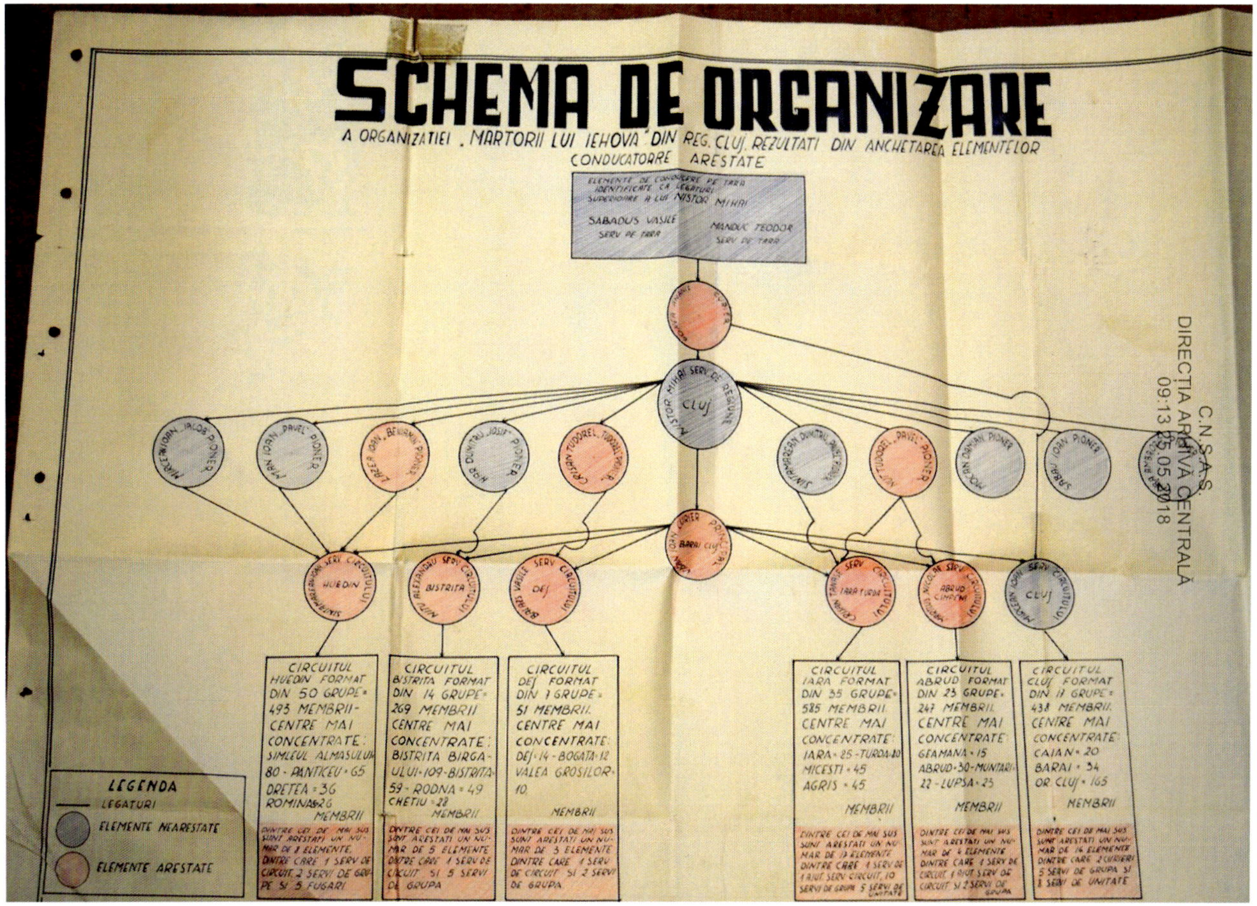

17.
Photo-Collage of Members of the True Orthodox Church
-
Tatiana Vagramenko

Photo-collages were another way to visualize dispersed religious groups as politically subversive networked organizations. This photo-collage was produced as part of an exemplary collective penal case against members of the catacomb True Orthodox Church (see entry 15). The top-secret document was published by the Soviet secret police in Voronezh in 1930. It was later sent to the Ukrainian OGPU, because numerous underground Orthodox communities were located in Ukraine. The secret publication was supposed to be a sort of textbook for use in the OGPU's campaign against the Catacomb Church. The instructions provided a structure, linguistic formulas and examples of political crimes to incriminate believers, all of which could be used to further the repressive measures taken against the True Orthodox Church in Ukraine.

This photo-collage groups images of repressed believers in one picture: thirty eight True Orthodox believers headed by Alexii Bui, bishop of the Voronezh diocese (top row, fourth from the left). The group on trial were mainly peasant believers as well as priests and monks from the Ukrainian and Russian countryside. Bishop Alexii (whose birth name was Semion Bui, hence the name Buevtsy that the secret police gave to his followers) was one of the important religious figures of the catacomb Orthodox movement. It was claimed that he united under his leadership communities of the True Orthodox Church in about forty districts in the southern provinces of Russia and in Ukraine. Alexii Bui was arrested in 1929 as the leader of the "counter-revolutionary ecclesiastical-monarchist organization of the *Buevtsy*." After several trials, he was sentenced to ten years hard labour and eventually he was killed by the NKVD in Sandarmokh, Karelia, on 3 November 1937.

Source

Digital Archive entry
http://hiddengalleries.eu/digitalarchive/s/en/item/8

ВАСИЛЬЕВА
ДУЛОВ
АРХАНГЕЛЬСКИЙ
БУЙ А.В.
БУТУЗОВ
СТЕБЛИН-КАМЕНСКИЙ
МАРЧЕВСКИЙ
КАСАТКИН
НИКИТИН
ПОЖАРОВ
ГУСЕВ
ПОЛЯКОВ
ПИСКАНОВСКАЯ
ВЯЗНИКОВ
ЯЩУК И.И.
КНЯЗЕВ
ГОРТИНСКИЙ
ЯКОВЛЕВ
КРЕЧКОВ
КАРЕЛЬСКИЙ
ЛИСИЦКИЙ
УВАРОВ
ЧИГАЕВА
ВЯЗНИКОВ
ШУМСКИХ
КОРЫСТИН
КАРЦЕВ
ТЫМЧИШИН
БИРЮКОВ
РЫЛЬЦЕВИЧ
ПИСКАНОВСКАЯ
ИВАНОВ
ВОСТРИКОВ
ВЛАДИМИРОВ
АЗАРОВ
СТЕПАНОВ
ГУСЕВ
ЗАВЬЯЛОВ
ШЕВЛЫКИН

CRIME SCENE PHOTOGRAPHS

The photographic practices of the police and secret police are remarkably similar across Central and Eastern Europe and are all based on models and principles devised and taught by Soviet officers. The photographic materials in secret police files, just like the texts amongst which they sit, were placed there with the intention of producing knowledge about the groups represented in order to incriminate them and exercise power over them. Towards the end of the nineteenth century, with the rapid advancement of photographic technology making it cheaper and more accessible, photography was very quickly adopted as a means to provide evidence to substantiate and elaborate written observations and reports. Photography early on became a tool of the police and state security, with photographs becoming invested with the status of proof. It also became one of the most important means by which the secret police could track their targets and gather convincing evidence of the activities and networks of those under surveillance. Through their internal magazines and work manuals, the secret police trained their officers both in the necessary technical requirements of the photographic operation, such as the equipment to be used in surveillance operations, as well as in the legal framework within which photographic evidence could be used. Photographs produced by the secret police fall into a number of categories, one of which is the crime scene photograph.

Crime scene photographs recorded the environment, context and circumstances of the crime for use as data for investigations and as evidence in the courts. They were, however, not considered as a suitable replacement by the secret police to a written description but rather as a supplement. Crime scene photographs can be broken down into a number of subcategories: the Environment Photo presents the general scene and background in order to understand how the perpetrators might have moved around the scene; the Overview Photo shows the exact place where the crime took place, demonstrating how different elements relate to one another; the Central Photo shows the key feature of the crime; and finally, the Detail Photo zooms in on small and important details, including the incriminating object or vital clues.

18. Forbidden Materials

\-

Ágnes Hesz

These crime scene photographs of Jehovah's Witnesses in the former administrative unit of Cluj in Romania were taken during various house searches conducted by the secret police (see also entry 16). The arrested leader of the Abrud circuit (a territorial unit within the Jehovah's Witnesses organization) is portrayed seated beside a glass jar containing coded reports. The picture appears to capture the moment when the jar was dug up from its concealment near the roots of a tree. Others images give close-ups of the material contained in the jar.

A "normal sized piece of firewood" found in the home of an arrested Huedin circuit servant (leader of the circuit responsible for coordinating congregation work within his unit) is shown with its inside carved out. Inside the police found the reports of the Huedin circuit from 1951 to 1954.

Another crime scene photograph shows a loudspeaker and accessories. The police found the loudspeaker in the well of the arrested assistant of the Huedin circuit servant, while other parts of the equipment were hidden piece by piece underneath a pigsty. According to the report, the loudspeaker was used during meetings. A coded report from the same circuit was hidden amongst unused tiles.

The photos follow the common standards of crime scene photography. Rather than being taken in the moment, the photographs are often staged in order to illustrate both the crime and the perpetrator. All the pictures in this case file were supplemented by detailed captions providing information about the items shown and the places they were found. The report included in the case file emphasized that Jehovah's Witnesses were exceptionally resourceful when it came to concealing forbidden materials, so much so that the secret police needed tip-offs from their informers to find them. The photos in this file were used to support accusations that were made against arrested members, including participating in a conspiratorial and hostile organization, producing and disseminating forbidden publications, encouraging young men to refuse military service and holding clandestine meetings.

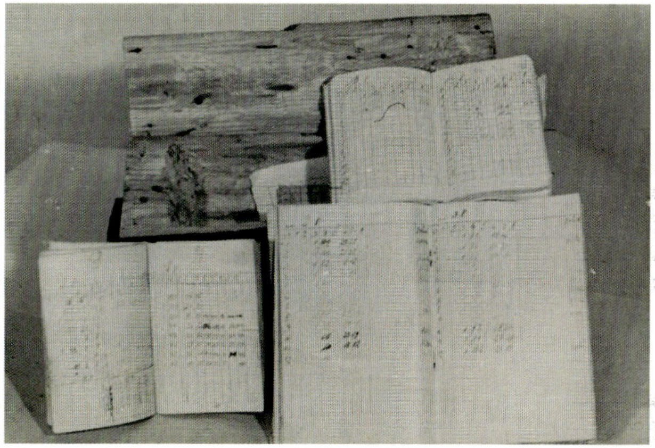

Source

Digital Archive entry

http://hiddengalleries.eu/digitalarchive/s/en/item/283

19.
Hieromonk Seraphim at the Scene of the Crime
-
Tatiana Vagramenko

In 1945 the police raided an underground monastery of True Orthodox Christians. It was located in a vault under a private house in the town of Chuhuiv, near Kharkiv, Ukraine. As a result, nine believers (most of them nuns and monks) were arrested with hieromonk Seraphim (Shevtsov) amongst them. All religious artefacts belonging to the community were confiscated and most of them were later destroyed. A series of photographs taken during the raid were later attached to a NKGB criminal file as incriminating evidence (see entry 2).

The religious items were taken out from the underground monastery and piled together, with father Seraphim seated next to them. The images show the confiscated church property at the same time inscribing the arrestee, father Seraphim, into the crime scene. In one photograph, father Seraphim sits surrounded by church utensils, antiminses and icons, whilst in another he is pictured with confiscated valuables and a clock.

Hieromonk Seraphim (1875-1955) was among thousands of monks left homeless when their monasteries were closed down by the Bolsheviks and who later joined the catacomb True Orthodox Church. He was a long-term leader of underground Orthodox churches and monasteries in northeast Ukraine. For several decades, Seraphim was the focus of close attention from the Soviet secret services, as he was seemingly the only catacomb priest in the region. A special secret operation called "Christoduls," which continued after Seraphim's death, targeted his clandestine communities of believers. Until the date of his second arrest on 11 July 1945, he hid in different underground monasteries and churches near the city of Kharkiv.

Seraphim was sentenced to seven years hard labour. He was released in 1952 and went into hiding again, continuing his "illegal" activities. In the following years, the secret police were busy searching for him, trying to recruit informers from inside his circle and raiding newly revealed underground churches and home communities. They did not know that Seraphim had died and had been secretly buried in one of the underground monasteries in 1955. According to the recollections of Seraphim's followers, the secret police eventually discovered Seraphim's grave and exhumed his body in order to prevent a growing pilgrimage movement. The body was unspoiled and the coffin emitted a fragrance of such strength that the police officers complained that a whole bottle of perfume had been poured inside.

Source
© State Archive Branch of the Security Services of Ukraine (Haluzevyi derzhavnyi arkhiv Sluzhby bezpeky Ukrainy-HDA SBU), fond 6-fp, spr. 75976.
Digital Archive entry
http://hiddengalleries.eu/digitalarchive/s/en/item/140

20.
The Typewriter
-
Anca Maria Șincan

The typewriter, and indeed any other equipment that could be used to disseminate information and proselytize (i.e. tape recorder, video recorder, video player), was considered a dangerous weapon that could be used against the regime and was amongst the clearest evidence to demonstrate the illegal creation, production and reproduction of materials. Here, Old Calendarist Bishop Evloghie Oța is pictured with the incriminating evidence of his anti-state activity, his portable typewriter. These two photographs appear in an evidence file of an underground Old Calendarist community in Bucharest (see entries 3, 10 and 52). In one photograph we see his typewriter placed near a Kalimavkion (Orthodox monastic headwear) visually linking the object with the owner. They are placed in the monastery dormitory on the bed, and what appears to be some literature is visible next to the typewriter. The other picture presents the owner of the typewriter with the open typewriter. The room is more visible in this image, and on the bed several leaflets and books are spread to reinforce the link between the person, the typewriter and the use to which it was put. It was common practice for the secret police to bring suspects back to the (crime) scene in order to produce staged photographs as incriminating evidence.

These types of images are recurrent in evidence files. Romanian legislation during the communist period specified certain regulations around typewriter ownership. Every typewriter was registered with the state administration and a page with the typewriter's letters and signs was kept in a police file so that typed documents could be identified by the typewriter they were produced on, and in this way linked to the owner of the machine (see also entries 22 and 31).

Source

Digital Archive entry
http://hiddengalleries.eu/digitalarchive/s/en/item/23

21.
Smuggling Books
-
Iuliana Cindrea

In September 1985 Romanian Customs Officers stopped and searched a car belonging to three tourists who were trying to cross the border into Romania. According to the report, they had been attempting to smuggle religious and other forbidden materials into the country. There is no mention of where the tourists came from; however, based on the registration plate of their car, which can be seen in some of the photos, it is safe to assume that they were West Germans from Karlsruhe. The tourists were fined and denied access to the country.

The police took a series of photographs capturing the officers uncovering the religious materials that were hidden in various hard-to-reach places inside the car, such as the engine area. The photos were taken at the precise moment (or were staged to appear as such) in an attempt to emphasize the dramatic character of the situation and to further incriminate the smugglers. The three tourists were also photographed together with all the religious materials that were hidden in their car. Among the books we can see a few Bibles, brochures, calendars, some cassettes and songbooks. These materials were confiscated along with the list of names of the people that they were supposed to be delivered to.

Source
© National Council for the Study of the Securitate Archives (Consiliul Național pentru Studierea Arhivelor Securității-CNSAS), D 00003, vol. 1.
Digital Archive entry
http://hiddengalleries.eu/digitalarchive/s/en/item/215

ISUS
RĂSTIGNIT PENTRU MINE
PAUL TUCKER

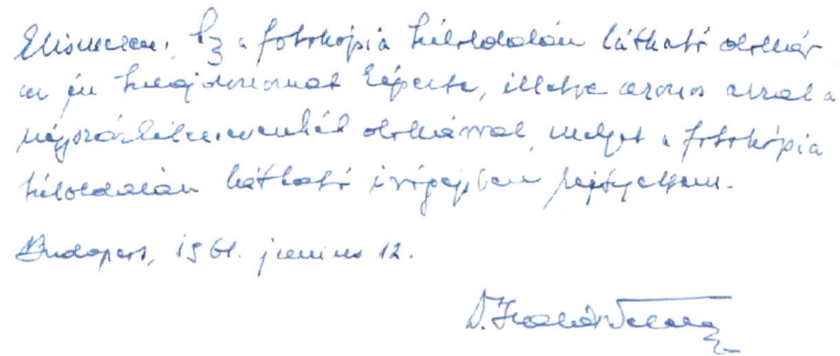

Elismerem, hogy a fotokópia hátoldalán látható dollár az én tulajdonomat képezte, illetve azonos azzal a négyszázkilencvenhét dollárral, melyet a fotokópia hátoldalán látható írógépjében rejtettem.

Budapest, 1961. június 12.

Dr. Halász Ferenc

22. Evidence against the Catholic Underground

-

Kinga Povedák

In 1950 most Catholic religious orders were dissolved in Hungary, with many priests and monastics choosing to continue their religious lives in secret as part of the religious underground. In 1961, the Hungarian authorities organized a show trial against the underground Cistercian order. Dr. Ferenc Piusz Halász (1909-1994), a Hungarian Cistercian monk, was among the main defendants in the show trial.

From 1946 he had been the Prior of the austere, ascetic Borsodpuszta Cistercian community. After the dissolution of his order, Dr. Ferenc Piusz Halász became a parish priest in Csatka from 1951 to 1961. The operation against him began in 1961. According to the charges against him in the show trial, he was one of the ideological leaders of priests and monks plotting the overthrow of the political system. During his allegedly subversive, anti-state efforts, he copied and reproduced a sermon collection titled "Preach the Gospel!" which served as evidence in the trial. Dr. Ferenc Piusz Halász was convicted and sentenced to six years in prison, but was freed in 1963 as part of the collective political amnesty. He was convicted again, however, in 1965 with a similar sentence.

These photographs served as one of the main pieces of evidence against Dr. Ferenc Piusz Halász. His Continental typewriter was confiscated during a house search. The typewriter was photographed along with illegally-held U.S. dollars. Three photographs were taken by the secret police in order to show how the U.S. dollars were hidden in an envelope inside the typewriter. On the reverse of the photograph we find the following text in Hungarian: "I acknowledge that the dollars on the other side of this photographic image are my property and are identical with the 497 dollars that I hid in my typewriter, which is found on the photo as well. Budapest, 12 June 1961. Dr. Ferenc Halász."

The sequence of shots demonstrates a classic photographic method used by the secret police in the production of evidence. In this case, we can assume that the dollars were planted by the secret police agents. Similar to show trials where the authorities have already determined the guilt of the defendant(s), the house search scenario was usually constructed in a way that the forbidden western foreign money—in this case U.S. dollars—was hidden and then found by the officers on the spot. The possession of foreign currency was considered a criminal offence, according to the state, and served as unambiguous evidence against the incriminated person. Likewise, typewriters of persons under surveillance had a significant role in the eye of the secret police, as unregistered typewriters could be used for the production and circulation of uncensored documents, messages or spiritual writings (see also entries 20 and 31). For this reason, the typewriter can also be seen as the symbol of free speech.

Source

© Historical Archives of the Hungarian State Security (Állambiztonsági Szolgálatok Történeti Levéltára-ÁBTL), 3.1.9. V-146835/3.

Digital Archive entry

http://hiddengalleries.eu/digitalarchive/s/en/item/4

THE UNITED STATES OF AMERICA

23.
Re-staging Ritual

-

James Kapaló and Dumitru Lisnic

Photographs taken by the secret police are not always what they seem. Here, the camera appears to capture a ritual performed by Archangelists, members of an Orthodox dissent movement from Bessarabia, in one of their many underground places of worship. On closer inspection, however, it is evident that this is not a surveillance photograph, but rather a staged re-enactment performed especially for the secret police lens. The framing, camera angle, lighting and mood of the photograph were all determined by the photographer with the intention of creating a powerful image for use by the regime. The two Archangelists, shown wearing ritual clothing and holding sacred objects, may not be performing a genuine ritual at all.

The images from this secret police photo shoot later appeared in the Moldovan press, such as the one shown here of the same two Archangelist leaders that appeared in *Tinerimea Moldovei* (Youth of Moldova), demonstrating the close co-operation between the secret police and the state media organs at the time. Re-stagings of religious ritual seem to have been produced consciously both as evidence for use in trials and as propaganda tools. With access to state security files on religious groups in postcommunism, researchers can now piece together the way that the secret police and Soviet public media and propaganda organs worked together to produce images of religion for popular consumption. The file in which these images appear contains numerous photographic materials from several cases and seems to have been made available to journalists and authors for use in their works.

Sources

Țopa, F. & Sibiriac A., Oameni vii cu suflete, *Tinerimea Moldovei, 09 March*, 1958.

Digital Archive entry

http://hiddengalleries.eu/digitalarchive/s/en/item/1

24.

Filming the Ioannites

-

Tatiana Vagramenko

In 1959 the Soviet secret police arrested father Mitrofan, a priest of an underground Orthodox community in Cherkasy region, Ukraine. Father Mitrofan was known among believers as a miraculous healer. The village of Osytniazhka where he lived attracted numerous pilgrims who sought his blessing and spiritual help. These images come from a KGB criminal case against him. The photographs portray father Mitrofan in his house, which had been turned into a clandestine chapel. He is dressed in Orthodox vestments against a background of icons, performing a religious service or talking to women, seemingly his followers. Another image included in the file records the ritual washing of feet, also performed in father Mitrofan's home. The photographs produced by the secret police, however, differ from typical secret police arrest or surveillance images. They intend to depict religious community life in an apparently natural context. At the same time, the good quality of the photos, taken with a bright artificial light, indicate that these representations of rituals were staged. The photographs are actually stills taken from a 1959 propaganda film, which was based on a show trial against father Mitrofan and his community. Apart from the records of the public trial, the film shows confiscated and later destroyed icons and religious manuscripts. It also shows staged rituals, gatherings and pilgrimages performed by the believers on trial.

The arrested believers were charged with being members of the True Orthodox Church. However, numerous confiscated images of father Ioann (John) of Kronstadt and manuscripts with the prophecy "The Dream of Father John of Kronstadt" attributed to him suggest that this was most likely Ioannite community. Ioannitism was a popular apocalyptic and chiliastic movement that emerged from the Russian Orthodox tradition at the beginning of the twentieth century. The Ioannites were mainly peasant believers from the Russian and Ukrainian countryside who venerated father John of Kronstadt (1829-1909), an archpriest from a town near St. Petersburg, one of the most popular religious personalities in late Imperial Russia. In the early Soviet period, the Ioannites were persecuted as harmful ecclesiastic-monarchist sectarians. Driven underground, Ioannite communities built clandestine chapels and continued to live as underground monastic communities scattered from western Siberia to Ukraine. Repression and a shared underground experience drew the Ioannites together with catacomb True Orthodox communities. In the later years, the Soviet secret services made no distinction between the Ioannites and the True Orthodox Christians.

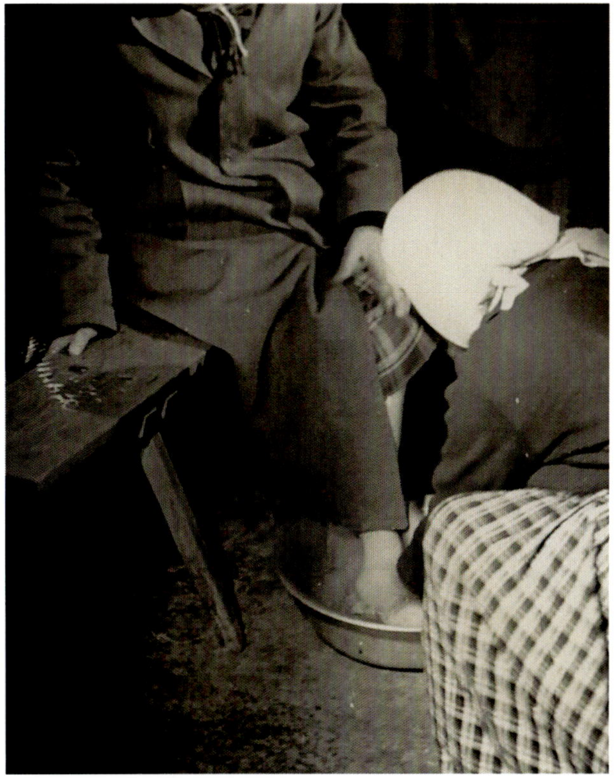

Source

Digital Archive entry

http://hiddengalleries.eu/digitalarchive/s/en/item/161

PHOTOGRAPH ALBUMS

The secret police developed several methods for representing and curating visual materials stemming from surveilled groups or persons. Photo albums represent one of these, although they were relatively rarely used compared to other means of archiving and ordering photographic materials. Some of the albums we find in the secret police archival collections were compiled by secret police officers and included both images confiscated from the target person/group and images created by the secret police (surveillance or crime scene photos, images of confiscated items). These compilations were more than just a handsome, practical way of ordering visual materials: they formed a carefully structured narrative to incriminate religious groups as dangerous and hostile to the regime. As well as photo albums created by the secret services, secret police archives also contain albums that were confiscated from persons and families. Containing family portraits or shots of family events, these albums were valuable for the authorities because they provided information on family relations and friendship networks, the life histories and the social backgrounds of their owners. The police could then use this invaluable information in its operational work.

ALBUM

5865

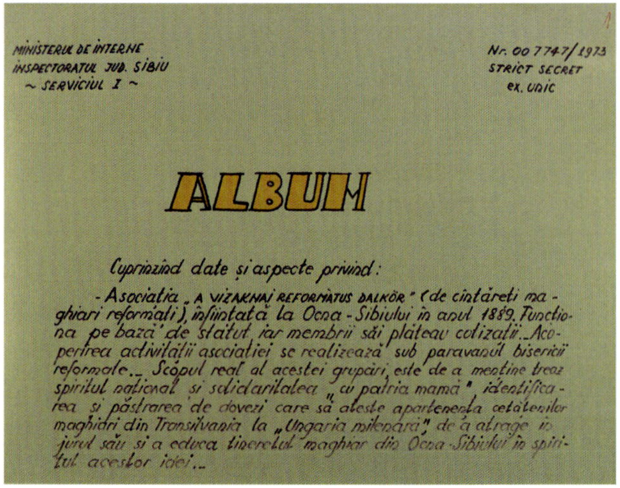

MINISTERUL DE INTERNE
INSPECTORATUL JUD. SIBIU
~ SERVICIUL I ~

Nr. 00 7747/1973
STRICT SECRET
ex. unic

ALBUM

Cuprinzind date și aspecte privind:

- Asociatia „A VIZAKNAI REFORMATUS DALKÖR" (de cintăreti maghiari reformati), înființată la Ocna-Sibiului în anul 1889. Functiona pe bază de statut, iar membrii săi plăteau cotizatii. Acoperirea activitătii asociatiei se realizează sub paravanul bisericii reformate. Scopul real al acestei grupări este de a mentine treaz spiritul national și solidaritatea „cu patria mamă", identificarea și păstrarea de dovezi care să ateste apartenența cetătenilor maghiari din Transilvania la „Ungaria milenară", de a atrage în jurul său și a educa tineretul maghiar din Ocna-Sibiului în spiritul acestor idei.

25.
A Hungarian Calvinist Church Choir in Pictures
-
Ágnes Hesz

When I first contacted the Hungarian Calvinist Church Choir in the town of Ocna Sibiului (Vízakna), Transylvania, after finding their file in the Romanian secret police archives, they were very welcoming, but warned me that I might not find much in their archive, because their documents "were stolen by the secret police." Sometime in 1973, a man of Hungarian origin approached the former secretary of the choir, who was also an amateur historian dedicated to preserving the memories of the local Hungarian past. The man said he was very much interested in the history of the community, wanted to help them and planned to write an article about their past. Posing as a committed Hungarian, he managed to earn the trust of the old secretary, who lent him his handwritten notebooks about local history. However, "his trust," as someone from the community told me, "did not give birth to trust": a couple of days later his house and the choir's meeting room was raided by the Securitate. During this raid, the police confiscated the choir's archive and memorabilia, which was kept in a green chest.

The Securitate accused the choir, which was founded in 1889, of nurturing nationalist-irredentist ideals behind the façade of their church activities and of being hostile to the socialist Romanian state. This claim was presented in a documentary file taking the form of a photo album. It was compiled by a Securitate officer, who was the very same person befriending the choir's ex-secretary. The album contains photographs of confiscated documents and images owned by the group as well as images shot by the secret police. It starts with a report on the history and activity of the choir, in which the reporting officer made every effort to portray it as a conspiratorial group connected to other equally dubious Hungarian organizations. He also claimed that it had a negative influence on the discipline of the local community. The album then continues with group photographs of choir members, exterior and interior photos of the group's meeting room focusing on its Hungarian patriotic decoration, crime scene photos of confiscated materials, selected operative documentation of the choir (minutes of meetings, financial reports, membership lists, etc.), its correspondence with past members or other organizations, musical scores and, finally, several pages taken from the confiscated notebooks written by the choir's former secretary. The photos are supplemented with explanatory captions that give translations of the documents or point to the nationalistic nature of the choir; for example, under the 1971 group photo the officer writes: "the colour of the (previously Hungarian national) flag is now black, the symbol of mourning, and the Hungarian tricolour is carried secretly in the hearts of the members."

The Securitate's attack on the choir is still part of the community's memory and oral history. Although nobody was arrested and the choir was not dissolved, the incident had a lasting effect on the group. Trust was broken within the community; people were aware that their activities were under surveillance and assumed that they still had informers amongst their ranks. Neither the chest nor the handwritten notebooks had ever been returned to the community. The old secretary of the choir later made efforts to compensate for this loss of their history by re-creating and re-writing some of the stolen notebooks.

Source

Digital Archive entry
http://hiddengalleries.eu/digitalarchive/s/en/item/228

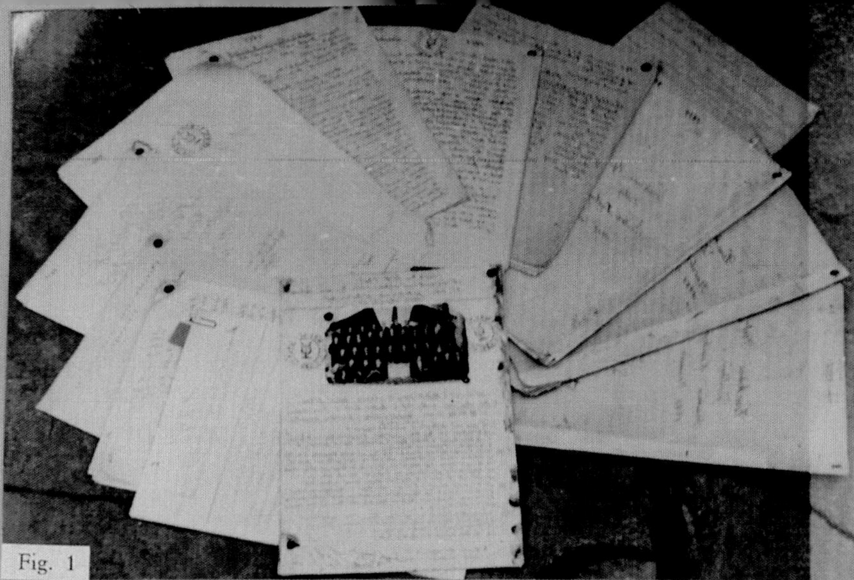

Fig. 1

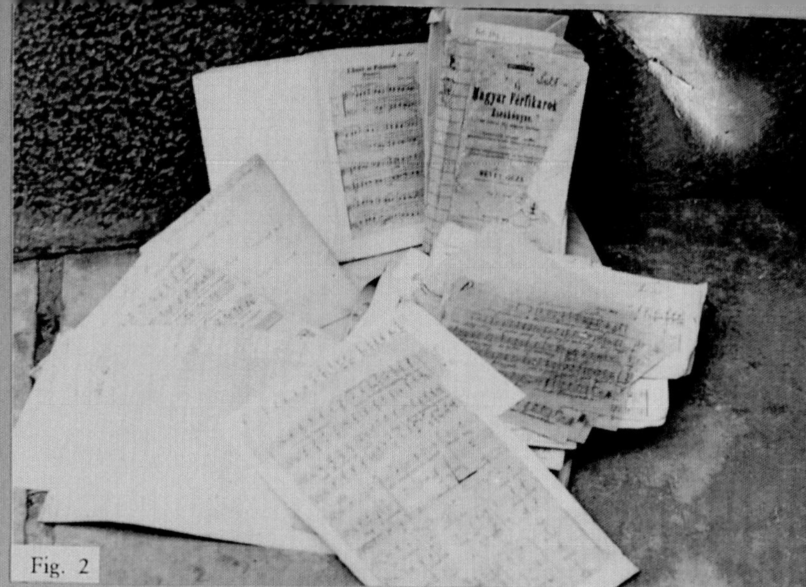

Fig. 2

Fig. 3

1. "Foi de amintiri", memorii ce conțin discursurile conducătorilor, date destinate pentru, generația viitoare.
2. Cărți și partituri muzicale cu conținut războinic și naționalist-iredentist.
3. „Amintire eternă pentru posteritate.
4. Pe capacul lăzii se află tabelul cu toți membri de rînd și conducătorii, precum și instrucțiuni privind păstrarea documentelor și destinația lor în caz de desfințarea asociației.

Fig. 4

26.
KGB Photo Album on Ukrainian Greek Catholic Leaders
-
Tatiana Vagramenko

The KGB in Krasnoyarsk published this photo album in 1958. It features arrested Ukrainian Greek Catholic Bishop Josyf Slipyi and two priests, Ilia Blavatsky and Vasyl Kavatsiv. Before it was moved to the secret police archive, the photo album had been kept in the internal "Chekist" library and seemingly served as an educational manual. It contains photographs of a police search with copies of confiscated manuscripts, correspondence and ritual items, as well as photographs of houses and barracks in the Siberian special settlements where religious leaders lived in exile following their release from prison. Seemingly, the photo album was based on the materials from a penal case against Josyf Slipyi, as most of the photographs place the police search of Slipyi's residence in the home for disabled people in the Krasnoyarsk region in 1958. The police search was followed by his arrest and a second term in prison in 1959. He spent in total 18 years in labour camps.

During the 1940s and 1950s, the organization of the Ukrainian Greek Catholic Church was virtually wiped out in the Soviet Union. The church was suppressed, as it was accused of being closely related to the Ukrainian Insurgent Army (UPA) and the Organization of Ukrainian Nationalists (OUN), both illegal in the Soviet Union. In 1945-46, the Soviet authorities initiated a forced reunification of the Ukrainian Greek Catholic Church with the Russian Orthodox Church, Moscow Patriarchate. Stalin signed the directive on the liquidation of the church and the secret police were placed in charge of the operation. As a means of intimidation, all Ukrainian Greek Catholic bishops, the metropolitan and over 800 priests were arrested during the liquidation campaign. Those clergy and faithful believers that refused the forced conversion to Orthodoxy were driven underground, forming the largest catacomb church in the Soviet Union. By the time of its liquidation, the Ukrainian Greek Catholic Church had four dioceses, one metropolitan, seven bishops, over 2,400 priests, 1,600 monastics and nearly four million believers, with only 30 percent of clergy having accepted the reunification with the Russian Orthodox Church. Believers and clergy were persecuted throughout the entire Soviet period, with thousands of them, including Bishop Josyf Slipyi, being deported to the Gulag. The church received legal recognition only in 1989 during Perestroika.

Source

Digital Archive entry
http://hiddengalleries.eu/digitalarchive/s/en/item/150

А-56

Близкая связь БЛАВАЦКОГО - националист КАВАЦИВ В.М.

СЛИПЫЙ И.И.
быв.митрополит греко-католической церкви.

БЛАВАЦКИЙ И.И.
бывший священник греко-католической церкви.

INVESTIGATIVE METHODS

The secret police in Central and Eastern Europe invested enormous effort and resources in their work against what seem to us to be marginal groups including even the smallest religious communities. From the 1960s onwards, the brute force of political repression of the 1930s, '40s and '50s shifted towards more subtle strategies of surveillance and control. Hundreds of thousands of secret police agents and informers were recruited to carry out endless surveillance and covert operations against "internal enemies." In order to obtain or produce criminal evidence, the secret police developed specific investigative practices and measures. Through their internal magazines, circulars and work manuals, the secret police trained their officers in various intelligence methods, such as eavesdropping techniques, the use of surveillance photography or cryptographic letters and cipher communication. Some of the most advanced technology for the time was deployed in operations, such as bugging telephone lines and apartments, using miniature photographic equipment, and microphones for external surveillance and eavesdropping. Intelligence operations against outlawed faith communities were often on a par with those directed against political dissidents and criminal gangs.

Source

Digital Archive entry
http://hiddengalleries.eu/digitalarchive/s/en/item/382

27.

Surveillance of the Greek Catholic Underground

-

Anca Maria Şincan

These two photographs come from a two-page collage representing Greek Catholic believers coming to underground services and meetings with Alexandru Todea, the underground Greek Catholic bishop in Reghin, Mureş county, in the mid-1960s. The images come from the informative file on Bishop Alexandru Todea that was opened upon his release from prison in 1964 as part of the general amnesty decree. The photo collage was sent by the Securitate officers from Mureş county to the central office in Bucharest with the description of the individuals represented in the pictures.

The pictures were the result of a longer period of surveillance of the visitors to the house where Todea was residing. They were classified and selected from a larger pool of people, categorized as those who often visited and those who seldom visited. The surveillance operation also identified the meeting places, either permanent or provisional (two houses and a place of work).

The two-page collage and the documents that explain it help us to understand the work of the Securitate in surveilling underground religious communities. For example, the photographed individuals are identified with aliases. In the description, they are identified with names, the names of parents, place and date of birth, current domicile and how many years the person attended school. Sometimes their employment history appears as well.

The focus in the description is also on gender and age. Men were considered more important in the underground religious communities, as they owned the houses where meetings and religious services took place. However, one can see from the collage that women made up the overwhelming majority of the visitors. The secret police also tracked the young men and women who participated, since they represented the future of the community and their resilience.

The majority of the people of the network were peasants or lived in the countryside, according to the description, but we can also see this from the way they are dressed; most of the women are wearing headscarves and aprons, whilst the man is wearing white trousers and shirt with a dark sleeveless overcoat and a traditional hat. Also, one can see in the pictures that the women carry large shoulder bags and baskets that are traditionally used to take goods to sell at the town market. These images also show the interest that the secret police had in the way the underground hierarchy of the Greek Catholic Church made their living, since they were not employed. They assumed, correctly, at least for the early years after their prison release, that peasants brought food to support their clergy.

28.
Meeting with a Secret Agent
-
Tatiana Vagramenko

After the annexation of western Ukraine in 1939, and particularly with the beginning of the Cold War, the Soviet state launched a full-scale attack against the Jehovah's Witnesses living in the western borderlands of the country (see also entry 4). The KGB carried out several secret operations that aimed at infiltrating the Jehovah's Witness leadership with KGB agents and informers. There were about 200 agents and informers working in the Witness underground in the Soviet Union in the mid-1950s.

In the summer of 1955, a group of Ukrainian Jehovah's Witnesses met clandestinely in the town of Morshyn, western Ukraine. They did not know that one of them had been recruited by the KGB as a secret agent. He was appointed by the secret police to meet with members of the Jehovah's Witness regional committee in Ukraine in order to gain their confidence and to intercept the communication channels of Ukrainian Jehovah's Witnesses with their headquarters abroad. During one of the meetings, the agent intercepted and copied the country missionary reports sent from Ukraine to the Polish Jehovah's Witness office and later submitted it to the KGB. The handwritten copies were attached to a surveillance file. A month later, two of the Witnesses from the meeting were arrested.

These photographs were taken with a hidden camera. They capture the meeting of a KGB agent with a group of Witnesses. Some photographs contain identification details on the reverse side: either the surveillance codenames of the photographed people, or their full names with date of birth and place of residence. We do not know who the secret agent was in these pictures. What we know is that in the following years, he became an important figure within the Witness organization. As a country committee member, he travelled abroad and established communication with the Witness centres in Poland and Switzerland. Many couriers smuggling information from the Soviet Union abroad were under his control. This is how the secret police obtained detailed and up-to-date information about the religious underground. The ensuing history of the Jehovah's Witnesses in the Soviet Union, however, shows that neither KGB agent infiltration nor mass deportation could prevent the community from thriving and steadily growing.

Source
© State Archive Branch of the Security Services of Ukraine (Haluzevyi derzhavnyi arkhiv Sluzhby bezpeky Ukrainy-HDA SBU), fond 1, op. 1, spr. 2677.
Digital Archive entry
http://hiddengalleries.eu/digitalarchive/s/en/item/373

29.

The Many Shadows of Bishop Dragomir

-

Anca Maria Șincan

These images come from the surveillance operation against the Greek Catholic Bishop Ioan Dragomir shortly after his release from prison in 1966. They all come from his personal file, which extends to ten volumes. The two collaged pages we see here are photographs taken in stake-out operations by Securitate officers from Maramureș county at the request of the central offices of the secret police. The officers had been instructed to map the network of persons Bishop Dragomir had contact with in his daily activities.

The first collage (on the left) is comprised of photographs where the camera is carried by the officer and is mobile and able to follow Bishop Dragomir after leaving his house. This page of images offers a visual story for the textual report submitted by the officer. One can discover, by looking at the photographs frame by frame, when the bishop leaves the house, who he meets, who he walks and talks with and the places he visits: the Roman Catholic parish house, the Roman Catholic Church, the market, the shop, the restaurant and the train station. The bishop was in most cases aware of the surveillance and thus he takes all types of precautions to hide his activity from the secret police officers. When the officer was close enough, dialogue was added to the visual material. The persons that the bishop met were one by one tracked down and also placed under surveillance. They are initially known by aliases in the file and gradually, as the officers learn more about the individuals, the file includes more thorough descriptions of their age, workplace and behaviour. You can see in the top photograph a meeting between Bishop Dragomir and one of the leaders of the former Peasant Party, Ilie Lazăr.

The second collage (on the right) is focused on the intimate daily activities of Bishop Dragomir. His family is tracked in their meetings with the subject and his visits to family members are recorded.

The final image comes from a third collage that captures Bishop Dragomir's funeral. The officers photographed the participants, counted them and then placed them under surveillance also. Bishop Dragomir was the oldest of the underground bishops and his funeral was an important event for the Greek Catholic Church; thus, the secret police followed it closely and recorded very minute details of the funeral ceremony and all those who attended.

Source

Digital Archive entry

http://hiddengalleries.eu/digitalarchive/s/en/item/385

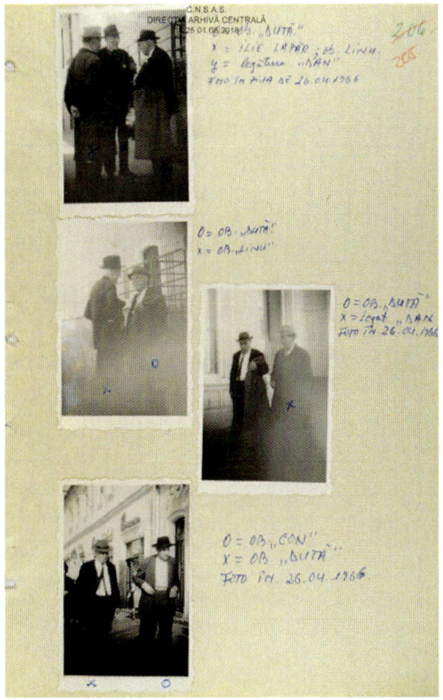

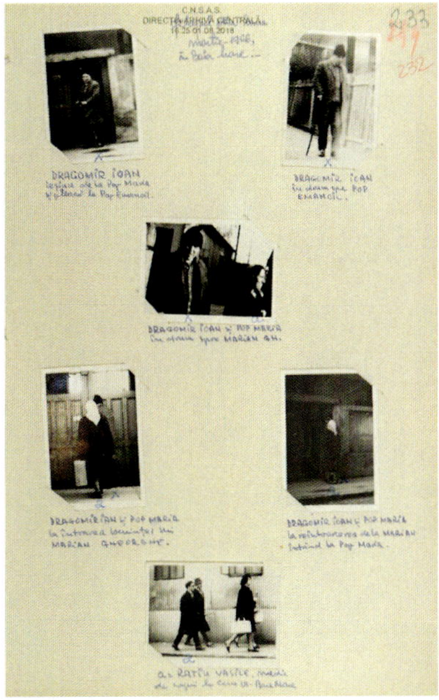

Анастас Иванович
МИКОЯН

Никита Сергеевич
ХРУЩЕВ

Лаврентий Павлович
БЕРИЯ

30. Defacing Soviet Leaders

-

Dumitru Lisnic

The Soviet regime had its own iconographic tradition, which aimed at dominating the gaze of Soviet citizens. Iconic portraits of the Soviet leaders were produced in massive quantities and distributed to every corner of the country. The mass-produced postcard-sized portraits of three Soviet leaders, Nikita Khrushchev, Lavrentiy Beria and Anastas Mikoyan, that we see here have all been torn. They appear as evidence in a secret police personal file, part of a collective penal case from 1953 (see entry 36). They were reported by the secret police to have been found during a house search of a believer in the village of Odaia in Moldova who was later tried as a leader of the Inochentist community. Inochentists were perceived as anti-Soviet sectarians who represented an obstacle to the projects of the Soviet state and were frequently accused of refusing the draft to the army, resisting mobilization for work on Sunday and refusing to vote in elections or to join the Communist Youth Organizations.

As with Eastern Orthodoxy more generally, the vernacular tradition of the Inochentists attributed a major role to icons. The intrusion of atheist Soviet iconography into the everyday life of villagers seriously disturbed Inochentist sensibilities. Later in the case file, a few days after Stalin's death, one of the witnesses reported having heard one of the Inochentist leaders saying, "why do you hang his portrait, is he a saint to be viewed by everyone, or what?" This case nicely illustrates the battle to dominate the gaze of the Soviet peasantry.

From the perspective of the secret police, the disrespectful attitude of those who had torn these pictures towards the above-mentioned leaders equated to an anti-Soviet act. The origin of the defaced images is open to a number of possible interpretations. Given the fact that the secret police officers claimed to have found these portraits in the attic of the Inochentist leader's house and the small size of the portraits, they may constitute fake evidence created by the secret police or somebody in collaboration with them.

However, the tearing of an image of any of the Soviet leaders would have been a risky strategy even for high-ranking secret police officers. The case file against the leaders of the community does not mention the torn pictures but instead translates the group's actions into the language of the Soviet criminal code. This file is a good example of how problematic the interpretation of secret police files can be and the ambiguity of some of the visual materials they contain.

Source

© Archives of the Information and Security Services of the Republic of Moldova (Arhiva Serviciului de Informații și Securitate al Republicii Moldova-ASISRM), 023171, Vol. 1-2.

Digital Archive entry

http://hiddengalleries.eu/digitalarchive/s/en/item/7

31.
Operation Leaflet
-
Anca Maria Șincan

Operation Leaflet (*Operațiunea Apelul*) was the code name the Securitate gave to the search for the individual or group of people that wrote a series of leaflets signed by the Committee for the Salvation of the Romanian Greek Catholic Church in 1977. The leaflets, which called for all Greek Catholics, Roman Catholics and friends of the Church to go at a certain hour on the feast of the Virgin's Ascension into former Greek Catholic churches and say a prayer so that God would grant president Nicolae Ceaușescu wisdom to legalize the Greek Catholic Church, were mailed to hundreds of addresses and spread to numerous Catholic communities, homes and churches, quickly papering the whole country. With the underground bishops and most of the more problematic voices amongst the Greek Catholic dissenters already under surveillance, the secret police were taken by surprise by this action, especially because they had no idea who could have penned the leaflet and orchestrated this operation. From that moment on, a huge sweep-up operation began. The Securitate interrogated all of their informers and all of the bishops and priests belonging to the Greek Catholic underground. They also reactivated all of their former informers and recruited new ones with the sole purpose of finding out who was responsible for this leaflet. For a long while they could not find anything, since nobody knew or was willing to talk about the identity of the Committee for the Salvation of the Romanian Greek Catholic Church.

The Securitate officers then changed tactics. They knew the post offices where the original letters had been mailed from, so they interrogated the post office employees and together with criminologists and a sketch artist they drew up several forensic sketches (*portrete robot*) with the likeness of the people who had posted the letters and leaflets. They also had the original typed leaflet and so they started to call in Greek Catholics, reactivating several databases of underground believers and clergy, to check their typewriter fonts so they could match the text to the typewriter the leaflet was written on (see also entry 20). This investigation took over seven years with enormous resources put into the operation. Several arrests were made before they narrowed the search down to Father Mihai Pop, a Greek Catholic priest from Cluj.

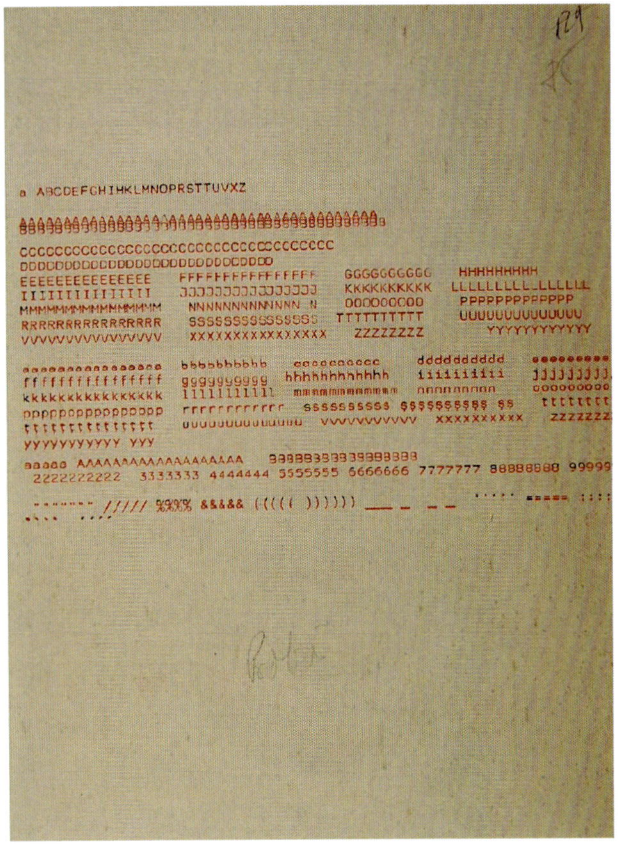

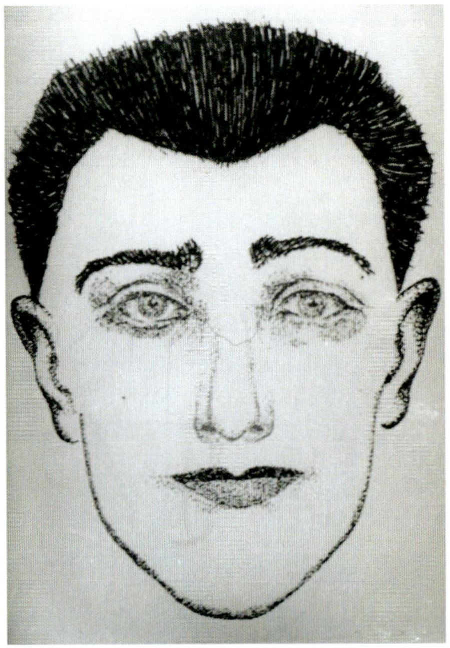

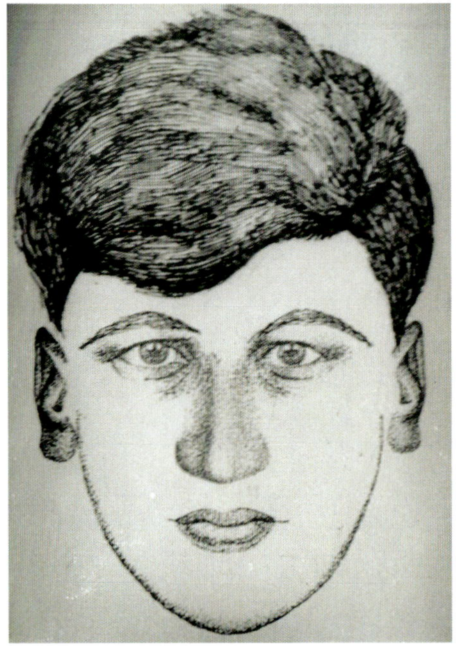

Source
© National Council for the Study of the Securitate Archives (Consiliul Național pentru Studierea Arhivelor Securității-CNSAS), D69, vol. 6, 10, 39.
Digital Archive entry
http://hiddengalleries.eu/digitalarchive/s/en/item/274

32.
Cryptographic Letters
-
Kinga Povedák

Agent "Géza Szebeni" was a Hungarian Baptist minister recruited in 1961 by the Hungarian secret police. In five working dossiers he reported on the inner life of the Baptist community in Hungary from 1961 to 1969. In 1969 he took up a position as the pastor of the Hungarian Baptist community in Detroit, Michigan. "Szebeni" was expected to work as an operative for a period of four to six years to "conduct research and maybe recruit people in addition to collecting, organizing and analyzing materials connected to the American small churches." From 1969 onwards he reported monthly through "first class cryptography." From the dossiers we learn that "Szebeni" was trained in intelligence methods, including the use of cryptographic letters for communication and in eavesdropping techniques and their prevention. The secret police produced a special instruction document titled "The basics of invisible cryptography" (*A láthatatlan tikosírás alapjai*) for agents such as "Szebeni."

The letters you see here were created using a cryptographic technique that allows the writer to hide the important message underneath a decoy message that contains inane and useless information. In this case, the cover letter resembles ordinary friendly correspondence such as family issues and weather. The cryptographic letter, which is hidden behind the cover letter and which had to be developed using a special technique, contained the intelligence information. One of the images shows a decoded transcript of the letters. The agent "Géza Szebeni" sent his letters to the Hungarian secret service using different Hungarian-American names and addresses. The officers of the Hungarian secret police kept reminding "Szebeni" to fold the paper first before writing to ensure that he did not write on the folded part, as it was not possible to develop text written in the fold. Often his coded messages were incomprehensible.

During 1969-70, "Szebeni" was met at a previously agreed location every six months; however, from 1971 reports from "Szebeni" become scarcer. He explains to his case officer that he felt he was under surveillance and therefore was not sending regular reports in order to protect himself. In 1972, the secret police broke off contacts with "Szebeni," as his existential and social situation took an unfavorable turn and his reports had no operative value for the Hungarian secret service. Finally, in 1976 he was expelled from the secret police network. When visiting Hungary in 1979 he returned his cryptographic toolkit, a black notebook. He died in 1981 in the U.S.A.

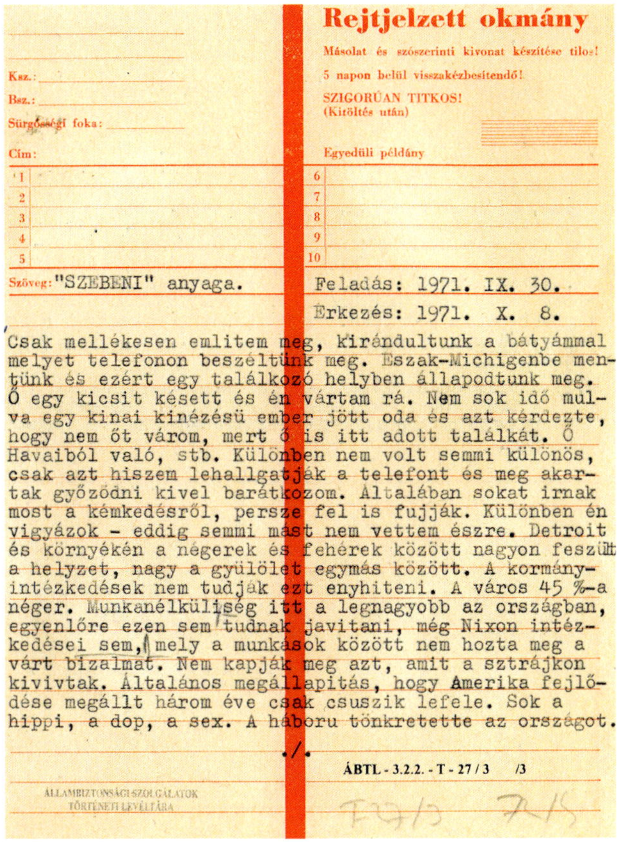

Rejtjelzett okmány

Másolat és szószerinti kivonat készítése tilos!
5 napon belül visszakézbesitendő!
SZIGORÚAN TITKOS!
(Kitöltés után)

Egyedüli példány

Ksz.:
Bsz.:
Sürgősségi foka:
Cím:

Szöveg: "SZEBENI" anyaga. Feladás: 1971. IX. 30.
Érkezés: 1971. X. 8.

Csak mellékesen emlitem meg, kirándultunk a bátyámmal melyet telefonon beszéltünk meg. Észak-Michigenbe mentünk és ezért egy találkozó helyben állapodtunk meg. Ő egy kicsit késett és én vártam rá. Nem sok idő mulva egy kinai kinézésü ember jött oda és azt kérdezte, hogy nem őt várom, mert ő is itt adott találkát. Ő Havaiból való, stb. Különben nem volt semmi különös, csak azt hiszem lehallgatják a telefont és meg akartak győzödni kivel barátkozom. Általában sokat irnak most a kémkedésről, persze fel is fujják. Különben én vigyázok – eddig semmi mást nem vettem észre. Detroit és környékén a négerek és fehérek között nagyon feszült a helyzet, nagy a gyülölet egymás között. A kormányintézkedések nem tudják ezt enyhiteni. A város 45 %-a néger. Munkanélküliség itt a legnagyobb az országban, egyenlőre ezen sem tudnak javitani, még Nixon intézkedései sem, amely a munkások között nem hozta meg a várt bizalmat. Nem kapják meg azt, amit a sztrájkon kivivtak. Általános megállapitás, hogy Amerika fejlődése megállt három éve csak csuszik lefele. Sok a hippi, a dop, a sex. A háboru tönkretette az országot.

./.

ÁBTL - 3.2.2. - T - 27 / 3 /3

ÁLLAMBIZTONSÁGI SZOLGÁLATOK TÖRTÉNETI LEVÉLTÁRA

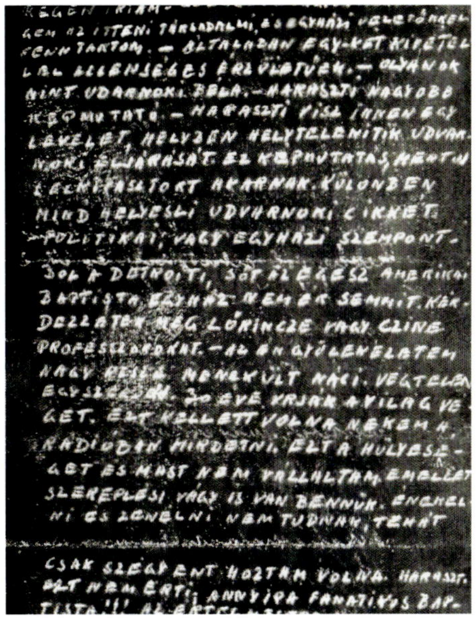

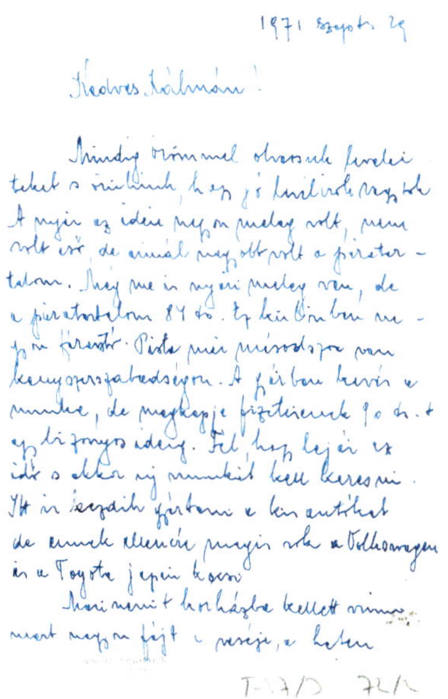

Source
© Historical Archives of the Hungarian State Security (Állambiztonsági Szolgálatok Történeti Levéltára-ÁBTL), 3.2.2 T-27/2-3.
Digital Archive entry
http://hiddengalleries.eu/digitalarchive/s/en/item/332

PART III.

CREATIVE AGENCY AND CULTURAL PATRIMONY

IMAGES OF RELIGIOUS LEADERS

The rapid development of photographic technology in the twentieth century resulted in new forms of religious visual expression. It made the production and reproduction of iconographic images more accessible to communities, both large and small, urban and rural, and offered them more creative possibilities. Groups were able to experiment and innovate, utilizing new techniques of photographic production, which in turn gave birth to new types of devotional image.

In Central and Eastern Europe, authoritarian regimes (sometimes in cooperation with majority or mainstream churches and denominations) attempted to regulate and control the production of non-sanctioned religious images, especially those of leaders who were not recognized by authorized religious institutions. In this context, the image of a religious leader could become a mark of creative resistance by religious groups.

Some groups developed icon-style photographic images of leaders persecuted by the regime reflecting their would-be saintly identity. Such photographs, which could be mass produced and easily hidden, became common in some contexts, especially amongst Orthodox dissenting movements.

The widespread use of images of religious leaders meant that they were often found on arrested believers. Such images were useful to the secret police as they could prove membership of illegal or banned groups and allegiance to unauthorized, underground leaders. Police officers could also try to identify the social networks through which the photographs were produced and spread. As a result, secret police investigation and case files contain numerous images of religious leaders found on arrested individuals that were used as evidence during trials.

Source

166

33.

A Postcard from Transnistria

-

James Kapaló

Inochentists, devout Orthodox followers of the monk Inochentie of Balta, enthusiastically embraced the creative possibilities that came with easy access to photographic technology and printing presses. Mass produced images of their leader in the form of postcards and photo-icons could be carried from village to village across the Moldovan countryside, easily concealed about their person.

This image was amongst the items confiscated when, in February 1942, the Romanian gendarmerie arrested a group of 41 Inochentists, nine men and 32 women, in an illegal "prayer house" in the village of Cuibușor, in Romanian-occupied Transnistria. This village was located adjacent to the underground Inochentist complex of Gradina Raiului (the Garden of Paradise) that had been destroyed by the Bolsheviks in 1920 and was on territory that had recently been occupied by Romania following the Axis invasion of the Soviet Union in June 1941. Now under Romanian control, many Inochentists began to return to the sacred sites associated with their now deceased leader in the expectation of the impending End of Days.

Inochentie appears here in a scene from his vernacular hagiography when he is under arrest, hands tied behind his back and surrounded by Tsarist soldiers, following his attempt to escape from exile on Solovetsky island—the notorious prison monastery in the Russian far north. On the reverse of the postcard there is a text that opens with an abridged and slightly altered version of Jesus' discourse on the Good Shepherd from John 10:14–16 which then goes on to equate the torments suffered by Inochentie to those of Christ's passion. "Here is the good shepherd whose life was given and is not given back. By his spiritual brothers, chased, cursed, shot [with a gun], insulted, given poison to drink, with hands tied behind his back, put in prison because he revealed the truth, not heeding what the Apostle says: whoever hates his brother is a murderer, and the murderer will not enter the Kingdom of God" (1 John 3:15). In this way, text and image were configured to establish a direct parallel between Inochentie's suffering and the passion of Jesus Christ. Both the postcard and the group's relocation to their sacred centre of the Garden of Paradise are expressions of the intensification of apocalyptic expectations of the group resulting from Romania's entry into World War Two.

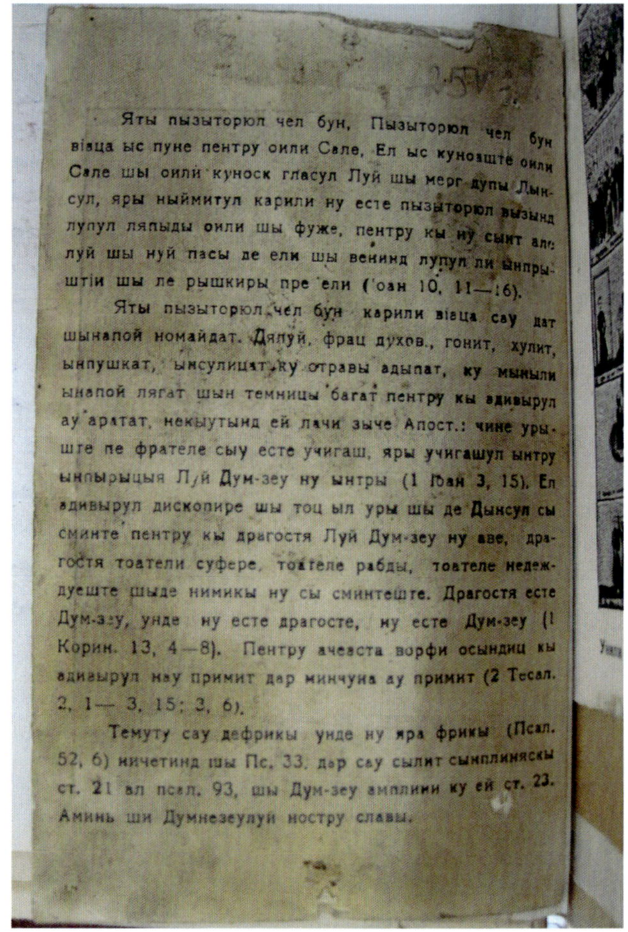

Яты пызыторюл чел бун, Пызыторюл чел бун віаца ыс пуне пентру оили Сале. Ел ыс куноаште оили Сале шы оили куноск гласул Луй шы мерг дупы Лынсул, яры ныймитул карили ну есте пызыторюл вызынд лупул ляпыды оили шы фуже, пентру кы ну сынт але луй шы нуй пасы де ели шы венинд лупул ле ынпрыштіи шы ле рышкиры пре ели (Иоан 10, 11—16).

Яты пызыторюл чел бун карили віаца сау дат шынапой номайдат. Дялуй, фрац духов., гонит, хулит, ынпушкат, ынсулицат, ку отравы адыпат, ку мыныли ынапой лягат шын темницы багат пентру кы адивырул ау аратат, некыутынд ей лачи зыче Апост.: чине урыште пе фрателе сыу есте учигаш, яры учигашул ынтру ынпырыцыя Луй Дум-зеу ну ынтры (1 Иоан 3, 15). Ел адивырул дископире шы тоц ыл уры шы де Дынсул сы сминте пентру кы драгостя Луй Дум-зеу ну аве, драгостя тоатели суфере, тоателе рабды, тоателе недеждуеште шыде нимикы ну сы смintеште. Драгостя есте Дум-зеу, унде ну есте драгосте, ну есте Дум-зеу (1 Корин. 13, 4—8). Пентру ачеаста ворфи осындиц кы адивырул нау примит дар минчуна ау примит (2 Тесал. 2, 1— 3, 15; 3, 6).

Темуту сау дефрикы унде ну яра фрикы (Псал. 52, 6) ничетинд шы Пс. 33. дар сау сылит сынплиняскы ст. 21 ал псал. 93, шы Дум-зеу амплини ку ей ст. 23. Аминь ши Думнезеулуй ностру славы.

Source

Digital Archive entry

http://hiddengalleries.eu/digitalarchive/s/en/item/13

34.
Postcards of Martyr Bishops
-
Anca Maria Șincan

In the 1970s the underground Greek Catholic community circulated photographs and devotional cards of its bishops that had refused the forced unification of their church with the Romanian Orthodox Church. The bishops seen here were all arrested, imprisoned and either died in prison or in forced domicile. These images show the Greek Catholic Bishops Ioan Suciu (d. 1953), Valeriu Traian Frențiu (d. 1952), Vasile Aftenie (d. 1950), Ioan Bălan (d. 1959), Alexandru Rusu (d. 1963), Tit Liviu Chinezu (d. 1955), and Cardinal Iuliu Hossu (d. 1970). Their photos have been collaged together and artistically framed around an image of the Greek Catholic Cathedral in Blaj. Because Cardinal Iuliu Hossu appears in the medallion with the date of his death, we can safely date the postcards to the 1970s. The photograph of an individual shows Bishop Ioan Dragomir dressed in his cassock with cincture and an episcopal cross. These visual clues serve to narrow the date when the postcards were produced to before 1985 when Bishop Ioan Dragomir died, since the file in which these images were found does not give any explanation of the postcard or the picture. The photograph and the postcard of the martyr bishops were used as a means to inform the community, through visual clues, that these bishops had died for their faith in the communist prisons and yet, nevertheless, the Church continues to live on in the underground.

Variants of these postcards can still be found in Greek Catholic communities, which suggests that they were widespread in the period and fairly accessible, and thus a useful method of passing information on the community through visual rather than textual means.

Source

Digital Archive entry
http://hiddengalleries.eu/digitalarchive/s/en/item/337

35.
"The Archangel Michael Looked Just Like Me"

-

James Kapaló

Alexandru Culeac, pictured here, was the leader of a religious movement in Bessarabia known as Archangelism. Included in a large collection of confiscated photographs, this photo-icon is one of three copies of the same image that appear in a Romanian Military Tribunal file from 1938. This photo-icon became an important devotional image for Alexandru Culeac's followers. In the image we see how techniques of montage and over-painting have been used to create a striking iconization of Alexandru Culeac, who is pictured with a flaming sword, a shield and a dove at his heart, a sign of his dual identity as both the Holy Spirit and Archangel Michael.

Later, during the Soviet period, media reports and propaganda publications continued to draw attention to the significance of the production and distribution of religious images for the success of the Archangelist movement (see also entry 38), whilst also ridiculing the crudity of their production. After a number of arrests and exile to the Gulag, Alexandru Culeac was forced to make a confession, which was published in 1959 under the title "Repentance of a Sinner." There he explains how important the icon that "looked just like me" was for his career, for the Archangelist movement and for the promotion of his divine status:

> I decided then to make an icon with my image. I commissioned it from a painter who painted the Day of Judgement and the Ascension of the Archangel Michael, as well as my ascension to heaven. The icon was a success. And the Archangel Michael looked just like me. I declared this icon holy. And it started here. People threw themselves down on their knees in front of the icon. They kissed it and prayed to it to heal them from illness. I don't know if the icon cured anyone but in exchange we received a handsome income. They brought us cereals, money, carpets and cattle.

Intended to portray Alexandru Culeac as a religious charlatan who fooled his followers into making offerings to him, this extract from his confession (which in all likelyhood was extracted under duress) nevertheless gives us an insight into the devotional power of this image preserved by the Romanian military courts.

Source

© National Archives of the Republic of Moldova (Arhiva Națională a Republicii Moldova - ANRM), fond Tribunalul militar al Corpului III armată, dosar. 738-1-6846.

Digital Archive entry

http://hiddengalleries.eu/digitalarchive/s/en/item/301

36.
The Mugshots of the Spiritual Fathers from Odaia
-
Dumitru Lisnic

The mugshot is one of the main visual materials produced by the secret police during their investigations. Together with fingerprints and personal information, mugshots connect the police image of the alleged enemy to an actual person, whom they show stripped of personal dignity and agency, often head-shaven, dejected, pensive and nervous. Mugshots are contained in almost all secret police criminal investigation case files and were produced according to a very precise set of rules, which makes them very similar from one case to another. Although at first glance they seem less interesting than other types of visual material, their use in fieldwork can bring unexpected results.

During a fieldwork trip to the village of Odaia in Moldova in the summer of 2018, we offered local believers the possibility of viewing the mugshots from the criminal case file of Dumitru Busilcov, Gheorghe Mârza and Ermolae Croitor, the spiritual fathers of the local community. They had been arrested in 1953, accused of organizing a sectarian commune of followers of Ioan Zlotea (a monk and holy man who attracted a large following in Bessarabia in the interwar period) and Inochentie of Balta (the founder of the religious movement commonly referred to as Inochentism), and of collaboration with German and Romanian authorities during the war, and were condemned to 25 years of labour camp. For these believers, the mugshot made the connection between the religious leaders they had known at home in the community and their identity as fabricated and archived by the secret police. The contrast between the mugshots in the file and the saintly identities and miraculous deeds of their spiritual fathers that had been handed down in stories about their time in the Gulag could not have been starker.

Showing such images to descendant communities entails certain risks that need to be carefully balanced. The mugshots, when viewed outside of their archival context, came to possess a new agency with the potential to be both traumatic and liberatory for the community. However, the continued enclosure of Communist-era anti-sect case files in the archives and their separation from and lack of accessibility for the targeted communities also has the potential to cause future harm to minority religious groups. The disclosure of archival images represents an important means through which the numerous propaganda myths about allegedly harmful sects can be deconstructed. Without the inclusion of the voices of members of persecuted groups, the analysis and re-interpretation of the textual and visual materials stored in the police archives will always remain incomplete.

Source
© Archives of the Information and Security Services of the Republic of Moldova (Arhiva Serviciului de Informații și Securitate al Republicii Moldova-ASISRM), 023171, Vol. 1-2.
Digital Archive entry
http://hiddengalleries.eu/digitalarchive/s/en/item/400

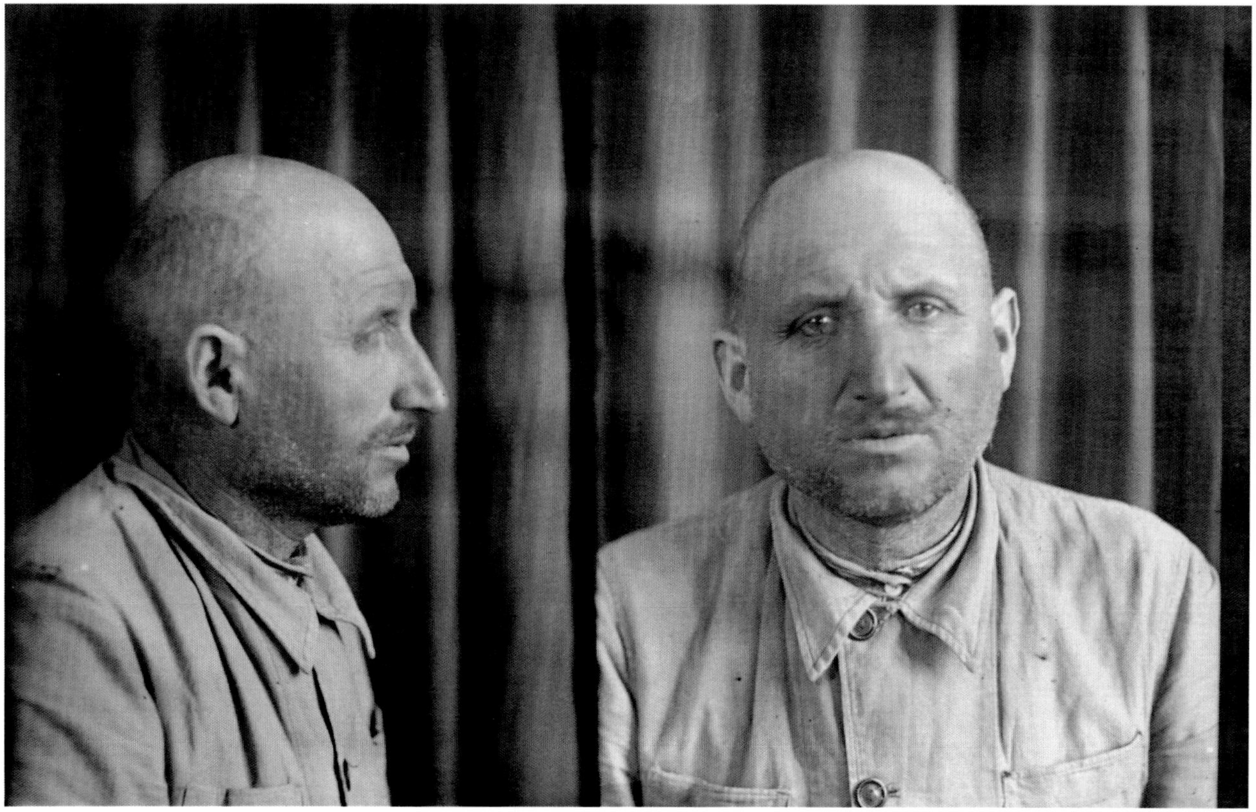

37.

The Mugshot as Devotional Image

-

Iuliana Cindrea

These mugshots were confiscated in 1952 by the Securitate from Onofrei V. Onofrei, a Romanian Old Calendarist monk, who was also the secretary of an Old Calendarist community. The mugshots of Glicherie Tănase, one of the most important Old Calendarist leaders, were taken in 1936 in Neamț county when he was arrested after the first confrontations between the Old Calendarists and the state authorities. He was arrested again in 1952 and numerous attempts were made by members of the group to set him free. According to the penal file of Onofrei V. Onofrei, described as one of the youngest members of the group and also as a mystical member, he obtained these mugshots from a militiaman who was working in Neamț county and managed to make copies of them at a photography studio in the same county. Even though this is a police photograph, it was later distributed as a devotional image.

Onofrei made 45 copies of the mugshots in an attempt to encourage the community to remember their imprisoned spiritual leader. He went on to distribute 25 of these images to the monks of Slătioara Monastery, the largest Old Calendarist monastery, and to other Old Calendarist believers. In the file, the police report that they managed to confiscate four copies, two of which were included in the file. However, other copies of the same image can be found in his second penal file. Onofrei's actions were considered dangerous by the state and seen as an attempt to agitate against the regime. He was arrested and measures were taken to locate and confiscate the rest of the copies of the photograph from all the individuals he had managed to distribute them to.

Source

Digital Archive entry

http://hiddengalleries.eu/digitalarchive/s/en/item/19

38.
Archangelist Women
-
Dumitru Lisnic

Photographs were an important and powerful tool for some underground religious communities. Archangelism, which emerged in 1920s Bessarabia, inherited the iconographic tradition of Eastern Christianity but developed modern creative photographic techniques including photocopying and photo collage (see entry 35). These photographs were confiscated by the secret police of the Moldavian SSR from a community of Archangelists in 1952.

In one image we see the technique of photo collage in which the creator has utilized a copy of an Orthodox icon of a female saint, replacing the face with a photograph of the face of Elena Culeac, one of the leaders of the movement who was venerated as the embodiment of the Mother of God. Above the image of Elena Culeac, there is some writing similar to that used on Orthodox icons that praises her as a saint and as an empress.

It was also common practice for Archangelist communities to take group photographs of women preachers. Here we see women dressed in monastic-style robes, holding icons and crosses in a stance similar to those seen in iconographic representations of saints and martyrs (see entry 9). These powerful images of women reflect the important role that they played in Archangelist communities. Unlike mainstream Orthodox Christianity, where only men can become priests, Archangelist women hold leadership positions and officiate at some religious services (see entry 23). Not all the women in these photographs, however, shared the same status. According to the police records, and as the images suggest, the woman who is seated in both of the group photographs held more authority. In one photograph her status is marked by a special headscarf and in the other by a handkerchief placed on her left thigh. Both the headscarf and the handkerchief are decorated with crosses.

These confiscated photographs were used by the police as evidence of the women's involvement in the illegal sect and as a means of identification of other members of the group. Through these photographs, the police tried to reconstruct the entire network of Archangelists in the south of the Moldovan SSR.

Source
© National Archives of the Republic of Moldova (Arhiva Națională a Republicii Moldova-ANRM), fond R- 3401, Inventar 1, Dosar 3716.
Digital Archive entry
http://hiddengalleries.eu/digitalarchive/s/en/item/248

БУКУРЭТЕ, ЫМЯЭРУТЯСЭ
ИЛЯНЭ!
13.

9.

C O N F I S C A T E D   P H O T O G R A P H S

Group and community photographs feature heavily amongst the corpus of confiscated images in the secret police archives. Such images were often taken at pilgrimages, religious festivals and special gatherings, and were a means for the community to materialize communal memory and present their values and beliefs in distinctive visual form. For the secret police, they were an invaluable source of information and a convenient means of tracing networks and personal relationships in the religious underground. Arrested members of groups could be forced to name individuals with whom they had been photographed. The secret police archives, therefore, represent an important resource for understanding how religious groups chose to represent themselves and how the totalitarian system used images of religious groups in order to identify, trace and incriminate their members. Consequently, photographs of religious groups in the secret police archives have a dual character as both religious justification and incrimination.

39.
Confiscated Old Calendarist Postcard
-
Iuliana Cindrea

This photograph, reproduced as a postcard, was confiscated by the police in 1936 from Pavel Caras, a former monk, who was wandering the villages of Bessarabia distributing these postcards to people.

The photo was taken during the 1930s in Albineț, Bessarabia, which was one of the most important centres of Old Calendarist activity during the period. It depicts the Old Calendarists from Albineț standing in front of their church, which appears to be under construction. The photo contains a small description in the lower right hand corner which states, "In memory of the Church in Albineț, followers of the old calendar," without mentioning the specific date or year when the photo was taken.

Even though little information is given about its context, there are small details that reveal important aspects about the community and about the event captured in the photo. We can see that one man holds a bucket in his hand, which may contain holy water, which would indicate that the community was celebrating the consecration of their church. In the photo we see an Old Calendarist priest who appears to have been responsible for the dedication of the church. Considering the opposition that the Old Calendarists were facing during the 1930s, the priest may either have been a local one or may have travelled to Albineț from a nearby village. It was common practice at this time for priests to move from one village to another, consecrating newly built Old Calendarist churches and houses of prayer. These activities were followed closely by the secret police.

Even though this photograph seems to depict a peaceful and relatively small community of Old Calendarist believers, the reality was that Albineț was considered one of the most suspect places in Bessarabia during the 1930s. The Old Calendarists in the area were deemed rebellious and dangerous, defenders of Nicolae Climovici and Ieremia Pletosu, two of the most important priests wanted by the authorities. According to the archival documents, the photo was used by the Old Calendarist church in Albineț as a propaganda tool in an attempt to attract new adherents.

Source
© National Archives of Romania (Arhivele Naționale ale României-ANR), fond Inspectoratul General al Jandarmeriei, D 25/ 1935.
Digital Archive entry
http://hiddengalleries.eu/digitalarchive/s/en/item/18

40.
Seventh-Day Reformed Adventist Community Photograph
-
Tatiana Vagramenko

This photograph was confiscated in 1948 by the Soviet secret police from a Romanian peasant, named Vasile Litvan, who was repressed as a follower of the Seventh-Day Adventist Reformed movement in Chernivtsi oblast (former Northern Bukovina), Ukraine. The photograph was included in his criminal file. It pictures a community of Romanian Adventists who are festively dressed, with some of them holding Bibles as a symbol of their faith. Apart from this photograph, the police also confiscated a notebook with religious songs handwritten in the Romanian language.

According to the file, Vasile Litvan was a poor, illiterate Romanian peasant who lived in the small village of Pripruttia all his life. He was born at the time when Northern Bukovina was part of Romania and he was baptized by a Romanian Adventist missionary in 1924. In 1931, following the teachings of missionaries from Transylvania, he joined the Reformed Adventist movement. Before the annexation of Northern Bukovina by the Soviet Union and during World War Two, when Romania temporarily regained Northern Bukovina, Litvan was twice sentenced for his beliefs by the Romanian courts. His third sentence, in 1948, was received from a Soviet court. This time he was sentenced to ten years in a labour camp. As evidenced from the file, the secret police also created a separate criminal case against 17 other of Litvan's fellow believers from his village, including his wife.

The Reformed Adventist movement, which had split from the Church of the Seventh-Day Adventists, was banned in the Soviet Union. Its followers rigorously followed the sixth commandment, "Thou shalt not kill," and therefore refused military service, obligatory in the Soviet Union. Most of the repressed Reformed Adventists in the Soviet period were charged for their refusal to serve in the Red Army and for so-called anti-Soviet activity and propaganda.

Source

Digital Archive entry
http://hiddengalleries.eu/digitalarchive/s/en/item/199

41.
The Appearance of a Saint
-
James Kapaló

In February 1965 the members of a sisterhood of Inochentist women were under investigation by the Romanian Securitate because of their links to a charismatic leader, a "Saint" with the initials C. A., referred to by his flock as the prophet Elisha. An informer, "Dan Gheorghe" (not his real name), who had either infiltrated the group or been recruited from within it, after a conversation with the sisters reported the following:

> She [one of the leaders of the group] told me that the militia man [who lived next door to her] got hold of a photograph of her with C. A. and M. and that if she is asked by the militia if she knows C. A., that she won't say no because the militia have the photograph, but if she is asked about other "brothers" in the group she will say nothing even if they cut her into pieces. I asked her how the photograph reached the militia and she told me that she was photographed together with those I mentioned above, then she sent the photograph to C. A. through the post and in this way the militia had made a copy of the photograph. (CNSAS I 237454, vol. 3, 57)

This short extract from the informer's report tells us a lot about the biography of this particular photograph, revealing how the image was produced by members of the community, how it was shared, how it was intercepted by the secret police and finally how it was transformed into incriminating evidence that could be used to identify members of the underground community. This case illustrates the significance of the text/image relationship, as the informer's report engages the photograph as evidence of the clandestine meeting between the sisters and C.A. The image, however, is in stark contrast to the text that describes it; the text incriminates and implicates the image in a conspiratorial narrative, whereas the intention of the producers of the image was to commemorate a significant act of devotion to the group's spiritual leader, which they preserved and shared despite the risk that the photograph posed to the community.

Source
© National Council for the Study of the Securitate Archives (Consiliul Național pentru Studierea Arhivelor Securității-CNSAS), I 237454, vol. 3.
Digital Archive entry
http://hiddengalleries.eu/digitalarchive/s/en/item/172

42.

"Shot by the Gendarmes"

-

Iuliana Cindrea

Taken in 1934 or 1935 in the village of Toporăşti in the county of Vaslui, Romania, this photograph depicts the funeral of two victims of the Romanian gendarmerie following an attack on their church and an attempt to arrest the community's priest. A few Old Calendarist believers are standing around the coffins of two people, a man and a woman. They have icons placed on their chests and we can see that three of the children present in the photo have their hands on the coffins, implying that this is their parents' funeral. There is a short note on the right edge of the photo that states, "Shot by the gendarmes."

A short text on the back of the photo describes the event as follows: "From the massacre in Toporăşti–Vaslui. Mother and father shot by the gendarmes of the former regime for this belief," referring to the Old Calendarist belief. It is unclear to whom the photo belonged or how it ended up in the file.

The events that happened in Toporăşti in 1934 are similar to the events in the village of Cucova (entry 1), and mark the beginning of a series of confrontations between the Old Calendarists and the gendarmes. Described as massacres, these attacks were meant to dissipate the Old Calendarist communities in the region. Even though it is not very clear what caused the incident in Toporăşti, it seems that the gendarmes surrounded the church in an attempt to arrest the Old Calendarist priest present there. Based on some archival documents and other sources, twelve Old Calendarists and four gendarmes were wounded and three Old Calendarists were killed during the confrontation.

Source
© National Council for the Study of the Securitate Archives (Consiliul Naţional pentru Studierea Arhivelor Securităţii-CNSAS), I 1075010, vol. 4.
Digital Archive entry
http://hiddengalleries.eu/digitalarchive/s/en/item/212

43.
A Confiscated Family Album
-
Dumitru Lisnic

Confiscated in 1940, the photographs in this album portray the intimate moments in the life of a family that attempted to flee the Soviet Union to Romania. For over a hundred years both banks of Dniester river were part of the Russian Empire until, in 1918, Bessarabia was united with Romania and the river became the frontier between two antagonistic states. The new border brought profound changes to the region but did not put an end to the personal ties between the people on the two banks of the river.

In the winter of 1940 a woman of Bessarabian origin living in Odessa tried to join her family that lived on the Romanian side of the frontier by crossing the frozen river Dniester. The border was frequently transgressed from both sides by people seeking a better life or escaping repression. The number of illegal crossings from the Soviet side to Romania increased during times of famine and during the collectivization of agriculture. Those wanting to flee from the country were helped by the people living in the border area who knew the best places to cross the Dniester. Many were arrested or even killed when trying to cross. The woman whose family album was confiscated by the Soviet secret police tried to cross the border with the help of a guide from the village of Nezavertailovca. They were both arrested and sentenced to five and three years of imprisonment respectively.

Family albums were of great interest to the secret police as the Communist Party's project of social engineering required extraordinary power over every citizen. The Soviet state was therefore very attentive to kinship relations, which from the regime's perspective could in certain cases undermine one's devotion to the state and the party. The album that contained the pictures we see here was found on a person who had relatives abroad and therefore could be used to prove the existence of cross-border networks that were perceived as dangerous and may have been used to identify other would-be transgressors. Likewise, family photographs could provide secret police with data regarding the past of arrested persons. They allowed the officers to identify places they had visited and to read any notes on the reverse of the photographs that revealed their personal feelings and attitudes.

Source

fond R-3401, Inventar 1, Dosar 595.
Digital Archive entry
http://hiddengalleries.eu/digitalarchive/s/en/item/238

S. Speia
147

44.

Clandestine Pentecostal Baptism

-

Kinga Povedák

These images were confiscated in the course of a house raid by the secret police on an underground Pentecostal community in Budapest-Pesterzsébet on 26 September 1972. The photos, twelve in total, had been taken by a member of the community named in the secret police file. The confiscated images were later used as incriminating evidence against the leading figures of the community, including pastor József Németh (entry 5). These photographs were later shown to the community during an interview, in the course of which Lilla Gere, the daughter of the pastor, pointed out that the girl being baptized in the picture is actually her and that the baptism took place in the garden of the hidden house church in a specially constructed font when she was 12 years old. She went on to recall the raid, describing it in the following terms: "It was a terrible feeling, how they searched and ruined everything and the brutal way they did so." Her family suffered from ongoing surveillance after the raid: "They put our house under such close surveillance that it was not possible for people to come in... not even members of our close family! Even this was prohibited."

Even though the raid and her father's arrest only resulted in a short suspended sentence for the pastor, their lives were drastically altered. The hidden house church was no longer used and due to ongoing surveillance, the community dissolved. Lilla's father, József Németh, only succeeded in planting a new community ten years later in 1982. The new community began to gather again in the same hidden house church. However, by this time pastor József Németh had become a member of the officially registered Free Christian Church (Magyarországi Szabadkeresztyén Gyülekezet).

Source

Digital Archive entry

http://hiddengalleries.eu/digitalarchive/s/en/item/15

CONFISCATED RELIGIOUS MATERIALS

Publications and manuscripts feature heavily among the religious materials found in secret police archives or itemized on lists of confiscated materials. Most religious communities in the twentieth century promoted their ideas through the publication of religious periodicals, pamphlets and booklets, which could be cheaply produced and easily distributed. Many of these items were published in short runs by local presses. Individual members of religious groups also produced handwritten copies of religious books, hymns, poetry, prophecies, homilies, heavenly letters, magical letters of happiness, as well as music scores that circulated within communities when published materials were not available.

During periods of totalitarian rule, state authorities tried to regulate or ban the production of such materials. The secret police intercepted materials sent in the post, confiscated them in house searches or uncovered them at the border when individuals attempted to smuggle them. Due to their generally small size, however, booklets and leaflets could be easily concealed. They were generally distributed through underground religious networks, both nationally and internationally; in some cases they were distributed and sold by colporteurs (salesmen of religious literature) on markets, on trains or at pilgrimages. Many of the religious booklets and pamphlets we find in the secret police archives, which had little value for mainstream libraries and archives, are extremely rare and cannot be found in other state collections. Some of these materials have immense value for the religious communities that were divested of their sacred materials by the state.

45.
A Novena for the Freedom of the Greek Catholic Church
-
Anca Maria Șincan

In the early 1970s, during a raid and house search on Father Aurel Leluțiu, secret police officers found a typed prayer titled "Novena for the freedom of the Greek Catholic Church." The prayer, however, was not included in Father Leluțiu's file, but was instead preserved in the secret police file of Bishop Ioan Dragomir. The Novena, a nine-day prayer exercise, appeals to the Virgin Mary to intercede with Jesus on behalf of Romanian Greek Catholics and calls for the recognition and freedom of their church. It asks the Lord to "not be late in breaking the chains of the bishops, priests and believers that remain faithful to the church." This prayer was considered problematic by the Securitate and is mentioned in several other files.

Like a number of other memoranda and leaflets produced by the Greek Catholic underground in the late 1960s and 1970s, this prayer was considered political as it focused on the tangible goal of easing the repression that the community was experiencing at the time. The prayer asked the Virgin Mary to "soften the hardened hearts of the state leaders [...] so they would not fight the [church's] activity and its resurrection from the underground where persecution has pushed us."

Several tropes that characterize the life of the underground Greek Catholic Church can be noted in this prayer: the church of the catacombs, the silent church, being bound in and breaking of chains and the erasure of the memory of the church from the history of the nation. These themes run throughout the underground samizdat literature produced by the Greek Catholic intellectual and clerical elite.

The prayer was typed and was circulated extensively with mention of this prayer appearing in Bucharest, Brașov and Cluj-Napoca.

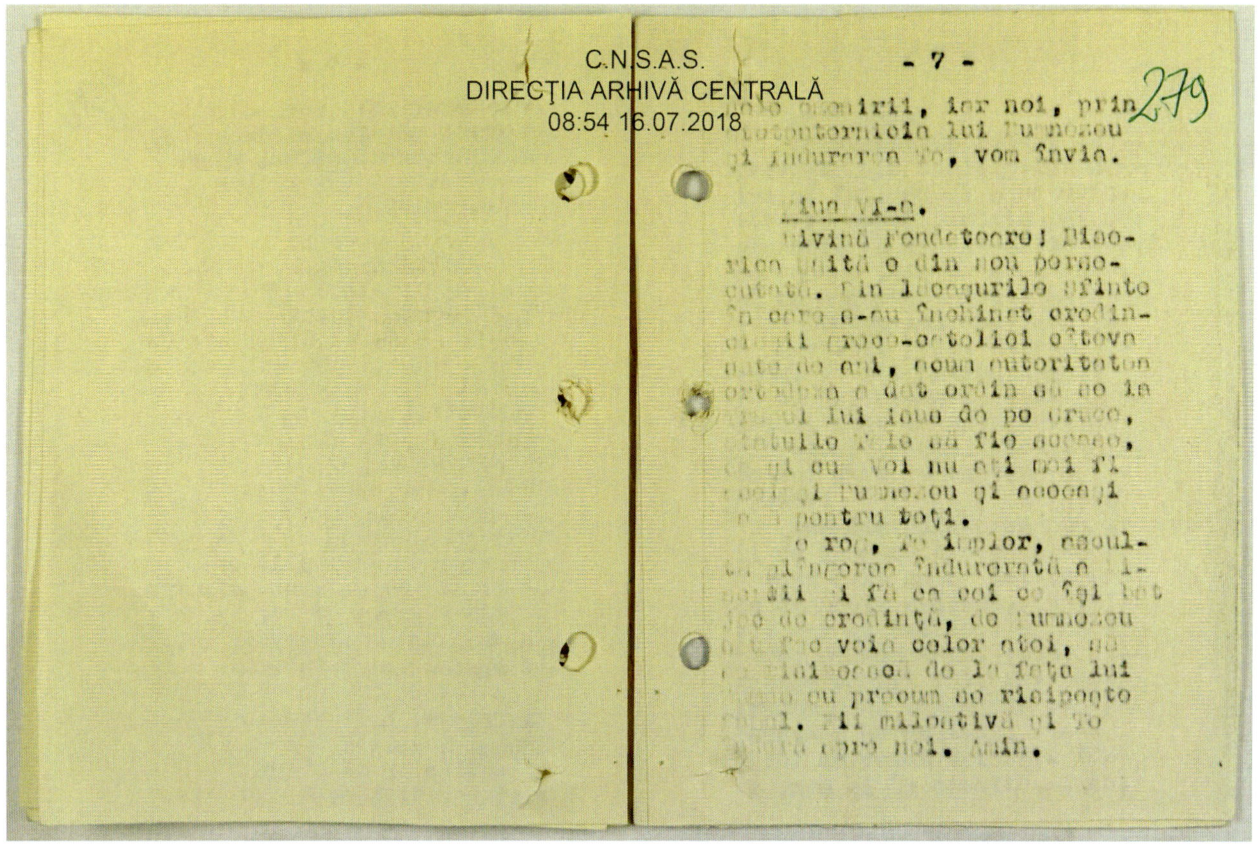

- 7 -
279
[illegible]irii, iar noi, prin
[illegible] lui [illegible]
[illegible], vom învia.

[illegible] VI-a.

[illegible]
[illegible] pentru toți.
[illegible] color [illegible]
[illegible] spre noi. Amin.

Source

Digital Archive entry
http://hiddengalleries.eu/digitalarchive/s/en/item/357

46.
Seventh-Day Reformed Adventist Confiscated Material
-
Tatiana Vagramenko

These images, dating from 1952, come from a criminal case against fourteen followers of the Seventh-Day Adventist Reformed movement in the provincial town of Bila Tserkva, Ukraine. Most of the arrested believers were poor, barely literate Ukrainian peasants who practiced their faith privately in their homes. All of them were found guilty of anti-Soviet activity and refusal of military service and were deported to the Gulag.

The photographs show religious manuscripts, books and photographs confiscated during their arrest that were carefully piled together to be exhibited at the trial. The legal judgement found the literature to have been "propagandizing religious obscurantism," being "ideologically harmful" and "alien to the Marxist-Leninist worldview." The original books and photographs were later destroyed (a list of confiscated items is included in the file). The photographs depict handwritten manuscripts and published books, confiscated journals with sheet music and nicely-framed, embroidered religious passages and citations from the Bible that were probably hung on the walls of their houses. Along with the pile of books and manuscripts, we can also see several photographs, including one picturing a collective baptism.

As evidenced from the file, believers passed the books to each other, sometimes copying them by hand before distributing them to others. During prayer gatherings, those who could read recited the religious literature to illiterate members of the community. Hiroaki Kuromiya, in his *Conscience on Trial: The Fate of Fourteen Pacifists in Stalin's Ukraine, 1952-1953*, gives a book-length account of how the arrested believers were tried. Through a close reading of pre-trial interrogation records, a closing indictment, court records and other documents included in the file, he shows that the case was heavily fabricated.

Source
© State Archive Branch of the Security Services of Ukraine (Haluzevyi derzhavnyi arkhiv Sluzhby bezpeky Ukrainy-HDA SBU), fond 6-fp, spr.58859.
Digital Archive entry
http://hiddengalleries.eu/digitalarchive/s/en/item/195

БЛАГАЯ ВѢСТЬ
ПРИИДИТЕ
КО МНЕ ВСЕ
ТРУЖДАЮЩИЕ
СЯ И ОБРЕМЕНЕ
ННЫЕ И Я УСПО
КОЮ ВАС
Я И ДОМ
мой будем
служить Госпо-
ду.

47.
Church of Turan Believers of One God
-
Ágnes Hesz

Mihály Virasztó had a long police record from both pre-communist and communist times, before and after 1945. As a priest (táltos) and missionary of the Church of the Turan Believers of One God, he was repeatedly sentenced to prison at the end of the 1930s for "agitation against religious denominations." He remained on the radar of the authorities in the communist regime for his anti-communist political views and activity, his relationships with right-wing figures abroad, and also for his past and supposedly present involvement with the Church of Turan Believers of One God. He had several clashes with the authorities: he was imprisoned for two months in 1952 for slander; detained for the possession of arms in 1957, a charge that was later dropped; his mental health was investigated and he was sent to a mental hospital in 1964 and 1967. After his last release in the summer of 1968, he was placed under the guardianship of his wife. His file was only closed in 1972.

The photos reproduced here come from a documentary file on Virasztó. They show the cover page of the Keleti Figyelő (*Orient Observer*), the short-lived journal of the Turan Historical Society founded by immigrant Hungarians in Melbourne, Australia, and a certificate of honorary membership of Mihály Virasztó for supporting the study of Hungarian history, issued by the same society in 1962.

The case of the *Orient Observer* is illustrative of the performative power of certain objects and of the responsive mechanisms of the secret police. By the time of the journal's arrival in February 1962, Mihály Virasztó had been under surveillance for years. The arrival of the journal and the certificate was reported by an informer in July 1962, only four months after the local county division of the secret police had claimed in a report that the Church of the Turan Believers of One God was practically non-existent in the region. The package set the machinery of the secret police in motion. The local branch of the secret police went to great lengths to get hold of the issues: they asked for photocopies from the Budapest headquarters, while also drawing up a plan to get Virasztó's own copies. The police also mobilized its network of informers to find out if Virasztó was disseminating the issues and instructed them to collect more information on the Turan Believers of One God. In September 1962, the Budapest headquarters sent the copies of the certificate and selected pages of the journal, with a short note that according to their examinations, the articles focused on "the origins and development of various languages."

The Orient Observer was founded in 1960 and had only two volumes and four numbers during its existence. Printed on a small offset printing machine and having hand-drawn illustrations, it claimed to be scientific and focused mainly on the origins of the Hungarian people. Although the articles were not openly political, the issues contained some negative references to communism and the Soviet Union. One of these, a sentence on the fatal consequences of Soviet dominance for the future of the Hungarian nation, was picked out by the secret police as proof of Virasztó possessing and circulating anti-communist content.

Source

Digital Archive entry

http://hiddengalleries.eu/digitalarchive/s/en/item/90

48.
Pentecostal Prophecy
-
Tatiana Vagramenko

Ukrainian Pentecostalism developed a particular culture of prophets who wandered across the wider region, preaching and gathering new communities. According to the Soviet authorities, during the 1950s there were approximately 200 unregistered Pentecostal communities in Ukraine with over 200 prophets and prophetesses.

This manuscript was confiscated in 1953 from an arrested Ukrainian woman who was known as a Pentecostal prophetess. The "wandering prophetess," as she was described by the MGB, led a Pentecostal community in Kiev and travelled throughout Ukraine and as far as Siberia, preaching to religious communities. She preached that Ukraine would become the Millennial Kingdom where all people would receive the baptism of the Holy Spirit. She was arrested in 1953 along with three other Pentecostal believers, all Ukrainian women, and sentenced to 25 years of hard labour. In 1937, the NKVD had arrested her husband, also a Pentecostal believer. The woman never heard from him again.

The prophecy is handwritten in a notebook and is 15 pages long. It narrates the coming death of Ashur, who will be cast down from his throne by God and will be shot dead. After his death, all the prisoners will be released and people will live in freedom. The prophecy also stresses a special religious role for Ukraine and Kiev, its capital, that will become a place of great spiritual awakening.

The manuscript with the prophecy was used by the Soviet secret police (MGB) as incriminating evidence of "anti-Soviet propaganda," including "dissemination of libel against Soviet leaders." The image of Ashur resembles Stalin: however, in one place in the prophecy Ashur is called Vyshinsky—the Minister of Foreign Affairs from 1949 to 1953 and one of the main organizers of Stalin's great terror, who signed thousands of death sentences in the 1930s. The following sentences in the text were underlined by an MGB officer, as supposedly having a distinct anti-Soviet meaning:

"And liberty [*volia*] and freedom will follow soon; the days of freedom are approaching. For Ashur will be overthrown. And people will be called. I will call up people from many countries, and they will arrive and will [condemn] Ashur. The end has come, they call Ashur to death, for Ashur will be shot dead. Oh, oh, oh the storm will arrive for there will come the great bloodshed..."

Source

© State Archive Branch of the Security Services of Ukraine (Haluzevi derzhavnyi arkhiv Sluzhby bezpeky Ukrainy-HDA SBU), fond 6-fp, spr. 60259.

Digital Archive entry

http://hiddengalleries.eu/digitalarchive/s/en/item/12

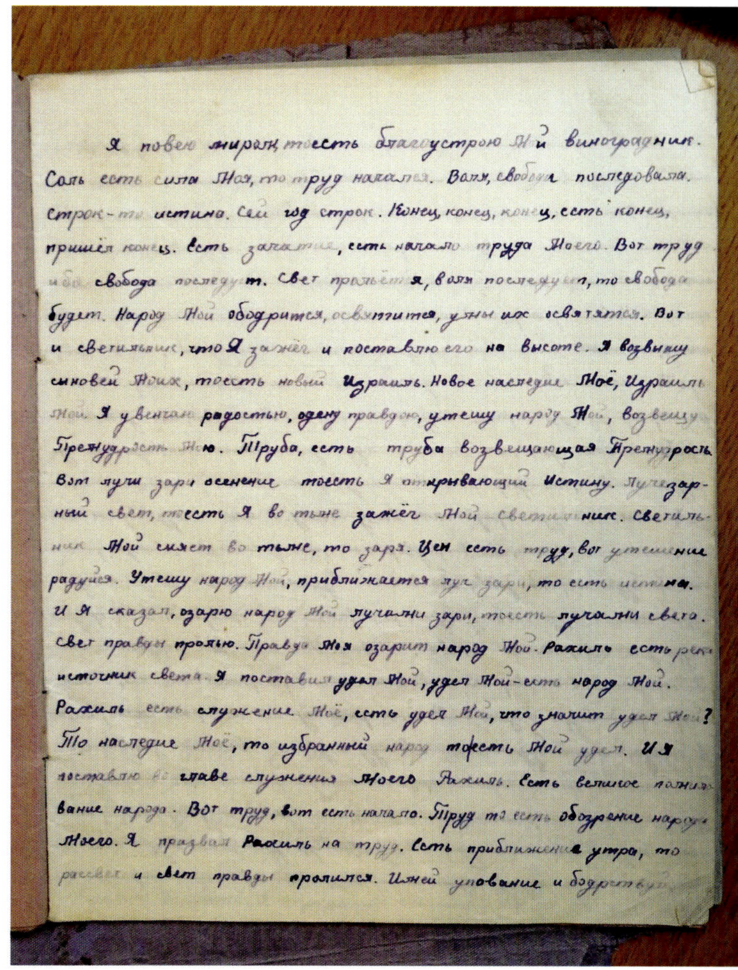

I.

Füzfő Angyala.

X.

A litéri sir ...

Magdi ! - Élsz Krisztusban ! ...

49.
"The Angel of Fűzfő"
-
Kinga Povedák

This typewritten book titled "Two towards one… III. Who was Magdi Bódi?" is an account of Mária Magdolna Bódi (1921-1945), a working-class girl from Balatonfűzfő, in which her life story is paralleled with that of the martyr St. Maria Goretti. Magdi Bódi was a young Catholic girl who had made a vow of chastity to Christ. She was active in organizing faith life in Balatonfűzfő, having initiated the local group of the Hungarian Catholic Working Women's Movement. According to the book, Magdi Bódi's parish priest instructed her to always keep a knife or scissors with her in order to be able to defend herself against the violence of the Soviet soldiers. In 1945, a Soviet soldier shot her as she was trying to protect herself from sexual assault. After 1989, a cult emerged around Magdi Bódi, especially in her home town where she was buried. Her beatification process was initiated by the Hungarian Catholic Church in 2017.

The samizdat book contains original photograph illustrations of Magdi, some with her family and one of her tombstone with a crucifix. In the dossier, the tomb of Magdi Bódi is discussed as a place of gathering of reactionary priests and sisters. The book features a photograph of Magdi Bódi. The caption below the image reads: "The Angel of Fűzfő." The images of the tomb of Magdi Bódi in the village of Litér has the following caption: "The tomb in Litér… Magdi! You live in Christ!"

The book was written by a Catholic abbot, Dr. Miklós Galambos, in 1955. He had heard of Magdi Bódi's martyrdom while imprisoned in Veszprém. The book is the third part of a series. The first two parts of the book series tell of the life of St. Maria Goretti. The content of the book is discussed in the dossier as anti-Soviet content in the guise of religion.

The book was confiscated from Dr. István Kiss, professor of theology and vice-director of the Theological College of Eger. He was the target of the operative dossier in which the book is located, as he was a representative in the Hungarian National Assembly for the Independent Smallholders' Party and had strong connections with the high clergy and democratic opposition leaders between 1945-48. The authorities judged him to be reactionary and he was under surveillance from 1951 onwards. Dr. Kiss was interrogated on several occasions from 1958 onward for spreading the illegal samizdat titled "The Angel of Füzitő."

Source

Digital Archive entry

http://hiddengalleries.eu/digitalarchive/s/en/item/327

PART IV.

FIELDWORK REFLECTIONS

Кондак 13.

50.
Echoes of Cucova
-
Iuliana Cindrea

It was January 2018, more than a year after the start of my archival research with the Hidden Galleries project, when I first caught sight of the photographs of Cucova in the secret police archives in Romania (see entry 1). Since then, these images that were taken as evidence of the so-called Old Calendarist rebellion of 1935 have become very important for my research, and I have spent long hours looking at them closely, exploring every detail to try and understand the event they depict.

Two years later, in November 2019, as part of the exhibition *Hidden Galleries: Clandestine Religion in the Secret Police Archives* at the Museum of Art in Cluj-Napoca, the story of Cucova greeted visitors with large reproductions of these photos covering the walls of the first room of the exhibition. Many of our research participants from the Old Calendarist church visited the exhibition for the opening and one of them began to tell me the stories that his grandfather had told him about Cucova and about the priest, Ioanică Dudescu. "Cucova was not his first encounter with the authorities," he said, "they once beat him and he lost a finger. Look, there, can you see it?" He pointed to one of the men in the photograph on the wall that showed arrested Old Calendarists lined up, sitting on chairs. There he was, with his hands on his knees, barefooted, dressed in civilian clothes, with nothing to set him apart from the other members except for a large "X" that the authorities had drawn next to him in order to identify him. The priest Ioanică Dudescu was, indeed, missing a finger.

Another detail about Dudescu from the images of Cucova was also affirmed for me by a member of the community. There is one photo that shows the exact place where he was reported by the authorities to have been found hiding, "dressed in women's clothes." At first I had thought this detail may have been made up by the police, but one member of the community told me that it was not uncommon: "No one cared about the women, so priests would sometimes dress in women's clothes to be able to slip past the authorities."

I had spent so much time staring at these photos and wondering about the relationship between the words of the police reports and the visual images they took to support the official version of the story. Reflecting back on these details, I would never have placed so much value on them as I did at that moment when all the elements converged in one place: the archive, the community, and a story that tied everything together.

Source

Digital Archive entry
http://hiddengalleries.eu/digitalarchive/s/en/item/3

Exhibition *Hidden Galleries: Clandestine Religion in the Secret Police Archives* at the Museum of Art in Cluj-Napoca, Romania. © Hidden Galleries project. Photo by Roland Vaczi.

51.
Tudorist Songbook
-
Iuliana Cindrea

I remember it was a cold day in October when I first entered the archives, sat down, asked for my files and began browsing the first one placed in front of me. It was an informative file; Name: Tudor Popescu, a former Orthodox priest, the founder of the Tudorist religious community in the early 1920s. The initial name of the community was the Scriptural Christians, but they soon became known as the Tudorists, after their founder. The group was outlawed for much of the interwar period, but in 1939 the Tudorists were forced to merge with the legally recognized Evangelical Christians. The Tudorists continued to have a distinct identity inside this larger group and are nowadays known as a second branch of the Evangelical Christians. The Tudorists rejected icons and many aspects of Orthodox tradition, and for this reason they were seen as a threat to both the Romanian Orthodox Church and the Romanian state.

At some point while browsing the file, I came across a songbook titled "Cântări creştinesti. 47." I didn't think much of it at first. Fast forward six months, and I'm sitting in a Tudorist pastor's house having an interesting conversation about the history of the community. Even though I was in my early stages of archival research, I thought I could show him some of the materials that I had already come across in the archives. I sent away all the thoughts that told me that what I had found was not good enough and I opened the files. He laughed, he smiled, he was dismissive of some of the materials, but then he stopped. "This is a very rare item," he said; I looked at the file and then I looked at him. It was the songbook. "Can I have it?" he asked. I smiled awkwardly, trying to find the best way of explaining why he is not allowed to have it. Not from me, at least. I apologized and told him that the legislation of the archives was quite strict regarding this issue, but that I could help him find out if he had a personal file. He was happy to hear that, but I felt guilty and everything about the situation seemed unfair. It felt as if I was confiscating that songbook all over again. I shook my head to make the thought go away, thanked him for the lovely conversation and left.

I later found out that the songbook was put together by Dumitru Cornilescu, a close friend of Tudor Popescu and an important religious reformer and translator of the Bible into the modern Romanian language. The songs were collected, translated and some of them composed by him in 1921, and were at first learnt by heart by the members of the community. Only later was Cornilescu able to collect them together and to publish the songbook. It had 47 songs and it remained the standard song collection for some years. The songbook that I found in the file was confiscated by the secret police sometime in the 1920s from two Tudorist women who were distributing brochures, calendars and other religious literature to people on the street. I don't know how many members of the community still hold a copy of the book or indeed if there are any other copies in existence. None of the members that I talked to owned one.

In October 2019 I mentioned the songbook again while interviewing a Tudorist believer from Târgovişte. He wanted to see it, and while he was browsing it, I heard him mumble something about how today the songs are not in the same order. He then smiled widely and said, "but today we have more than 400 songs. Can you believe it?"

Source

© National Council for the Study of the Securitate Archives (Consiliul Naţional pentru Studierea Arhivelor Securităţii-CNSAS), I 259046.

Digital Archive entry

http://hiddengalleries.eu/digitalarchive/s/en/item/20

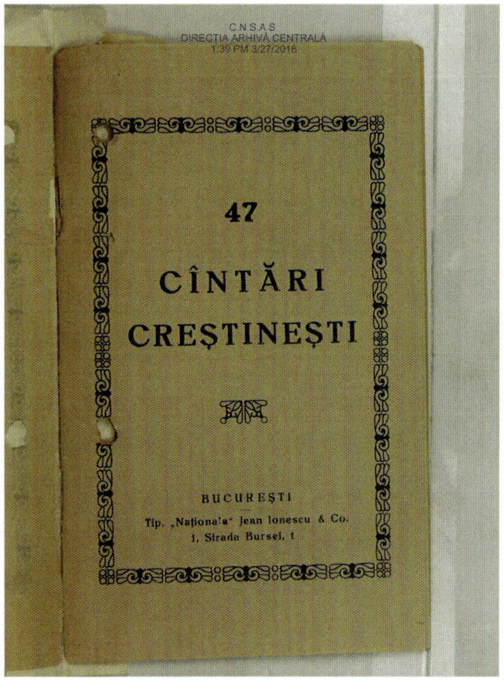

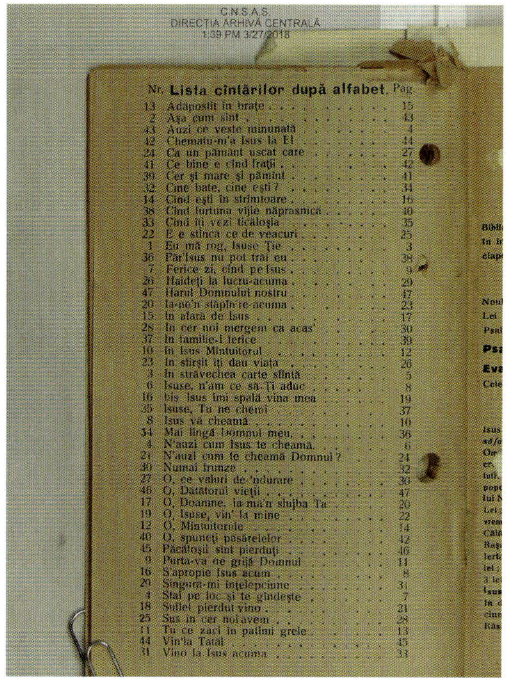

52.

Bishop Evloghie and His Prayer Beads

-

Anca Maria Șincan

Ever since the death and subsequent exhumation of the remains of Old Calendarist Romanian Orthodox Bishop Evloghie Oța (see entries 3 and 10) by the Romanian secret police, members of his Church have been searching for his remains. In February 1979 the Old Calendarist Orthodox Bishop Evloghie Oța died and was buried in a grave under the altar of his clandestine church on Televiziunii Street. In 1983 the secret police in a sweep-up operation meant to destroy the underground Old Calendarist community, arrested the monks and tore down the church and the monastic complex. In the process they also exhumed the body of the bishop that was buried underneath the altar of the church. The believers and monks were forbidden to return to the site.

After several stories from the bishop's file were uploaded on the Hidden Galleries Digital Archive, the community contacted the project. From this point on, I was able to gather several descriptions of Bishop Evloghie Oța's interment in his clandestine monastery from surviving witnesses. My interviewees described him as sitting on the bishop's throne, dressed in episcopal vestments, holding the Holy Scripture and the prayer beads. As I continued my ethnographic research with Old Calendarist online communities and two monasteries in Bucharest and Sibiu, photographs matching this description started to come to light. I first came across the photograph featured here on a Facebook group called *Imagini de Arhivă ale Bisericii Ortodoxe de Stil Vechi* (Archival images of the Old Calendarist Orthodox Church) where it had been posted by Sebastian Hriscu, who had tagged the image with the description, "picture found in my grandmother's archive." Discussions with Sebastian revealed that this picture of the bishop before he was interred by his monastic brothers inside the underground church in Televiziunii Street in February 1979 had circulated widely in Old Calendarist communities throughout the country after the bishop's death. The picture was not included in Oța's secret police file. Nevertheless, it fitted perfectly the description that comes through from the file documents and from the reports of secret police informants. I later acquired two other scanned copies of the same image from the monks at the Monastery *Adormirea Maicii Domnului* (Dormition of the Mother of God) in Bucharest, where Bishop Evloghie Oța was initially buried.

Today, the whereabouts of the body of the bishop remains unknown. However, in the photograph of Bishop Evloghie Oța we can see that he is holding a string of prayer beads, called *metanii*. These beads found their way into the possession of Bishop Flavian Bârgăoanu, who lives in what is now a thriving Old Calendarist Orthodox monastery in Televiziunii Street. In an interview from April 2019, he explained how the beads had been buried with Bishop Evloghie Oța and were then lost when the bishop was exhumed and his body and everything he was buried with were taken away by the secret police. A few months after the fall of the communist regime in Romania in December 1989, when he and several monastic brothers returned to Televiziunii Street, he received an unexpected visit from a man who had helped the secret police dig up of the body of Bishop Evloghie Oța. He brought with him the prayer beads and told Bishop Flavian that they had been on the body and he had taken them away and that so many bad things had happened to him subsequently that he now wished to return them to the monastery.

Sources
Bishop Flavian loaned Evloghie Oța's religious beads for the project's exhibition *Hidden Galleries: Clandestine Religion in the Secret Police Archives* at the Museum of Art in Cluj-Napoca, Romania, where they were displayed next to the picture of the body of the bishop before his internment. © Hidden Galleries project. Photo by Roland Vaczi.
The description of the burial of Bishop Evloghie Oța and the details of his interment can be found in the case file from National Council for the Study of the Securitate Archives (Consiliul Național pentru Studierea Arhivelor Securității-CNSAS), I161963, vol. 1.
Digital Archive entry
http://hiddengalleries.eu/digitalarchive/s/en/item/402

53.
The Stolen Stamp
-
Ágnes Hesz

"The stamp should come home. It should come home. The stamp and the sceptre and the crown always stay with the king."
"The stamp. It's a pity that that stamp was lost because, how should I say it, it was a document, really."
"A value."

This conversation was recorded during an interview in 2018, in the small town of Ocna Sibiului (Vízakna). The two men, father and son, were talking about the official stamp of the town's Hungarian Calvinist Church Choir, which had been confiscated during a secret police raid in 1973 along with the choir's archive. Documents and photographs confiscated from the choir were compiled by the Securitate into a photo album (see entry 25), which includes the president of the choir's celebratory speech (shown here) performed at the choir's eightieth anniversary. As with many of the group's documents, it bears the official stamp of the choir.

Although the choir was allowed to operate after the raid, as present members say, it was "robbed of its past," since none of the confiscated items were returned. Some attempts were made to compensate for this loss: for example, several documents were recreated by the choir's former secretary who, in lieu of the missing stamp, created a hand-drawn replica when necessary. The other image you see here was taken during ethnographic fieldwork in 2018 and shows a document with a hand-drawn replica of this stamp. Copying the stamp by hand was one way in which the choir coped with the loss of their belongings: in this case the loss of the choir's recorded history and an important symbol of its legitimacy, its stamp.

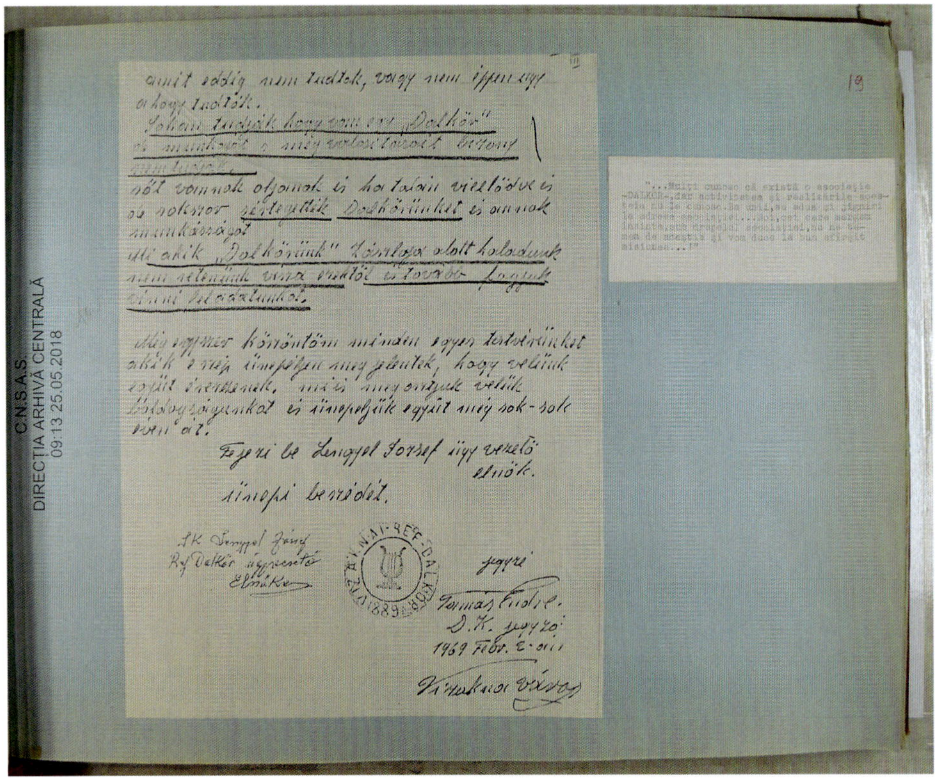

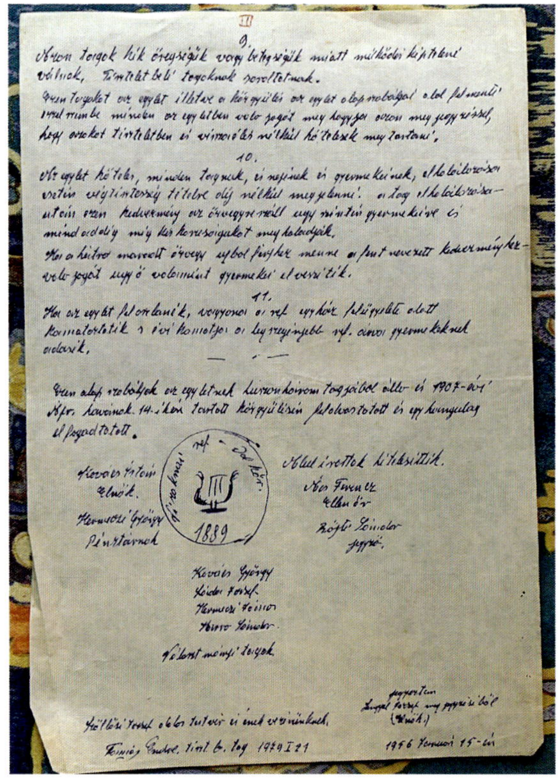

Source
© National Council for the Study of the Securitate Archives (Consiliul Național pentru Studierea Arhivelor Securității-CNSAS), D 015847.
Digital Archive entry
http://hiddengalleries.eu/digitalarchive/s/en/item/233

54.
A Story without a Case File
-
Kinga Povedák

During the course of the research that led to this publication, we approached several religious communities to discuss their presence in the secret police archives and the images and texts we found there. Although the majority of people we spoke to were very happy to engage with us and our research, we encountered some religious communities that were reluctant to speak and that decided not to engage with us. Feelings of distrust of authorities and state institutions have remained high in some communities, which, in part, is due to their experience with the secret police during communism.

As researchers, we are especially concerned with the ethical questions that arise regarding the legacy of repression and surveillance that we find in the archives, and as such decided to respect the decision of one particular community that was not willing to share their experience of their encounter with the secret police with us. Even though the guidelines and legal framework regarding the publishing of secret police archival materials would, in this instance, have allowed us to use images of this community without their consent, we decided that the most appropriate ethical response would be to respect their intention that these images remain unpublished and not researched. The establishment of mutual trust between the researcher and the researched community is at the heart of the ethnographic process. It is particularly important, therefore, to reflect on this "failed" ethnographic attempt as an indication of the lingering distrust in institutions, authorities and researchers in general as one of the legacies of repression and surveillance in the twentieth century.

Drawing from the Hidden Galleries exhibition Faith-Trust-Secrecy at Galeria Centralis, Blinken Open Society Archives, Budapest. © Dániel Kophelyi

POSTFACE

Exhibitions as Tools to Think With: On Impact and Process

-

Gabriela Nicolescu

Unlike the introduction, the postface to this catalogue is in the pleasant position of addressing those who have already looked at the images and who have read the entries, and who presumably found them interesting enough to make it this far. But this postface is not about the end of a book or of a project but rather about a beginning. Of what? One can wonder. In this postface, I want to talk about how research projects that include exhibitions in their making allow not only for knowledge to be built collaboratively and in an interdisciplinary way but also about a continuation of the impact of the research, the exhibition process and the way stakeholders look at things after the end of the funding.

In February 2018 I came into contact for the first time with the materials accumulated by members of the Hidden Galleries team. I remember I came to visit Cork and, in the company of most of the members of the research team, I was shown, projected on a big screen, anti-religious propaganda movies from Soviet times and images found in the many archives in Romania, Hungary, Republic of Moldova and Ukraine. While I was listening and asking questions about the stories of repression from twentieth century Central and Eastern Europe, I realized how fascinating this collection was. The visual and non-visual materials contained many paradoxes relating to what kind of information one can find in the archives and the complex and fragmented nature of the stories told. My contribution to that early meeting took not only the form of questions and suggestions, but of introducing to members of the team the idea, which I have explored elsewhere (Nicolescu 2016), that exhibitions can work as devices that can be used in situations of conflict and that they have a processual nature.

Seven months later I was employed to work on the project as Curatorial Lead, being in charge of using the collected materials to design four exhibitions in four different venues: the Museum of Art in Cluj-Napoca, Romania; the Open Society Archives in Budapest, Hungary; University College Cork, Ireland; and The National Museum of Ethnography and Natural History in Chișinău, Republic of Moldova. As a curator and visual anthropologist who has experience of doing research in archives, I started to look not only at the images collected, but also at what researchers in the project found "shiny" while spending months and years in the archives. This was the same principle used by Kathy Ferguson (2008) in her description of the research process in the archives: that while searching for illuminating things, meaning those things that stir up the imagination, those who enter the archives are provoked to make their own connections and to dream. Together with James Kapaló, we gathered recurrent themes and recurrent types of images, which later were transformed into curatorial concepts that were used in constructing the displays. With the researchers, we drew on their ethnographic encounters with members of the communities they researched, asking questions about the usefulness of revisiting archives, or of making their stories public; we asked for other images or objects that could be used for the displays.

The project team's ethnographic work also resulted in the presence of communities in the exhibition. In the images you see here, there are members of the Calvinist choir from Ocna Sibiului and Old Calendarist Orthodox monks from various monasteries in Romania, all of whom participated at the launch of the exhibition in Cluj. Some saw their presence at the launch as a symbolic reparation of past traumatic events. Others, with whom research was conducted, preferred to step back. All these encounters with people and objects, documents and memories helped us explore ways in which different stories could be made visible, but also ways in which difficult or problematic visual material could be shown in more subtle ways, or only referred to while not displayed at all. Questions of authenticity, partiality, trust, the ethics of making visible (and public) different specters of reality were recurrent in our discussions, especially in the context of our exhibitions, which bring new and different forms of visibility than the published work you hold in your hands.

In the making and opening of the exhibitions, the reality of exhibition as process became more evident. As researchers Cindrea, Hesz and Șincan underlined above, while having the images blown up on the wall, a different encounter with the visual material took place. Differently from a printed book, an article or an on-line posting, large (or smaller) prints on a museum wall allow for a bodily proximity and for a new type of knowledge to emerge. In the Museum of Art in Cluj-Napoca, visitors were able to notice the facial expressions of people in the photographs (be it pain, joy, or nonchalance when the camera was hidden and they had no clue they were being photographed), to experience similitude with relatives that came to visit the exhibition, to see more closely the bare feet of some peasants, a missing finger, the recurrence of the same cheaply produced paper icons on a wooden altar. All these details, presented closer to their and our eyes, made both visitors and researchers understand new and fresh things. We aimed to let the images speak for themselves, but we also introduced some labels, both long and short, about icons in museums, underground spaces and hiding techniques (encountered both among communities and the secret police), police aesthetics and last, but not least, a difficult cultural patrimony: the images and objects confiscated from some religious groups and never returned. When we did not know the answer, we were not afraid to ask questions.

Exhibition *Hidden Galleries: Clandestine Religion in the Secret Police Archives* at the Museum of Art in Cluj-Napoca, Romania. © Hidden Galleries project. Photo by Roland Vaczi.

To continue the idea of exhibitions as processes, the exhibition making was paralleled by a series of film projections, lectures, seminars and collaborations with high schools and universities, and by an online presence through various social media. Different reactions from members of the public, collected in discussions but also through feedback cards, helped us realize the innovatory dimension of the project and of the materials shown, but also point to where improvement could be made. Ideas on how to create impact once the exhibition was closed made us re-think the borders of the museum. From the encounters with different publics, we learned. It is exactly this aspect that makes us realize that the impact of the project is not yet finished, but only just started.

I end this postface by drawing on Derrida's (1998 [1995]) ideas on the two paradoxical forces that co-exist in archives (love and death). On the one hand, looking at this catalogue's entries or visiting the exhibitions, we witness how archives and archivists preserved and cared (voluntarily or not) for some stories to reach us in the present; the materials are still with us, and in the present we can reinterpret their many layers. On the other hand, one can witness how archives themselves were (and very often still are) instruments of power in the hands of all those who control them or have access to them. In the past they worked as proof and the tool for the destruction of certain people, or of entire religious communities. In many of the entries in this catalogue and in their display in the exhibitions one can find both forces at work. This catalogue is a catalogue of the digital archive, but through permutations and associations, it is also a catalogue that can be associated to any re-making of the exhibition in different venues and contexts. It allows for re-visits and for new interpretations. It is in this paradox that the power of the project resides. The idea is to make readers and visitors curious and allow them to search for more information in and beyond catalogues, archives or gallery spaces.

References

Derrida, Jacques. 1998 [1995]. *Archive Fever. A Freudian Impression.* Chicago: University of Chicago Press.

Ferguson, Kathy E. 2008. "Theorizing Shiny Things: Archival Labors." *Theory and Event* 11 (4): 3-7.

Nicolescu, Gabriela. 2016. "The Museum's Lexis: Driving objects into ideas." *The Journal of Material Culture* 21 (4): 465-489.

Lidia Guzy; James Kapalo (Eds.)
Marginalised and Endangered Worldviews
Comparative Studies on Contemporary Eurasia, India and South America
2017, 268 S., 29,90€, br., ISBN 978-3-643-90644-1

Tomáš Glanc; Zornitza Kazalarska; Alfrun Kliems (Eds.)
Performance – Cinema – Sound
Perspectives and Retrospectives in Central and Eastern Europe
2019, 230 S., 39,90€, br., ISBN 978-3-643-91081-3

Cosmin Budeanca; Dalia Báthory (eds.)
Histories (Un)Spoken
Strategies of Survival and Social-Professional Integration in Political Prisoners' Families in Communist Central and Eastern Europe in the '50s and '60s
2018, 394 S., 49,90€, br., ISBN 978-3-643-90983-1

Sorin Radu; Cosmin Budeanca (Eds.)
Countryside and Communism in Eastern Europe
Perceptions, Attitudes, Propaganda
2020, 798 S., 69,90€, br., ISBN 978-3-643-90715-8

Eugenia Roussou; Clara Saraiva; István Povedák (Eds.)
Expressions of Religion
Ethnography, Performance and the Senses
2019, 296 S., 39,90€, br., ISBN 978-3-643-91110-0

Clara Saraiva; Peter Jan Margry; Lionel Obadia; Kinga Povedák; José Mapril (Eds.)
Experiencing Religion
New approaches to personal religiosity
2016, 240 S., 39,90€, br., ISBN 978-3-643-90727-1

Raluca Mateoc; François Rüegg (Ed.)
Recalling Fieldwork
People, Places and Encounters
2020, 256 S., 39,90€, br., ISBN 978-3-643-80247-7

Andrea Friedli; Aline Gohard-Radenkovic; François Ruegg (Eds.)
Nation-building and Identities in Post-Soviet Societies
New Challenges for Social Sciences
2017, 280 S., 39,90€, br., ISBN 978-3-643-80218-7

Hana Horáková; Andrea Boscoboinik; Robin Smith (Eds.)
Utopia and Neoliberalism
Ethnographies of rural spaces
2018, 256 S., 29,90€, br., ISBN 978-3-643-80215-6

Sonja Schüler (Ed.)
Exchange, Dialogue, New Divisions?
Ethnic Groups and Political Cultures in Eastern Europe
2016, 192 S., 29,90€, br., ISBN 978-3-643-80209-5

Enriketa Pandelejmoni
Shkodra
Family and Urban Life (1918 – 1939)
2019, 298 pp., 34,90€, br., ISBN-CH978-3-643-91017-2

Detelina Tocheva
Intimate Devisions
Street-Level Orthodoxy in Post-Soviet Russia
2018, 240 pp., 29,90€, br., ISBN-978-3-643-90873-5

Ethnologia Balkanica

Klaus Roth (Ed.)
Emotions, Senses and Affects in the Context of Southeast Europe
Part 1
vol. 22, 2020, 248 pp., 29,90€, br., ISBN-978-3-643-91319-7

Klaus Roth; Milena Benovska (Eds.)
Balkan Life Courses
Part 2: Kinship, Religion and Memory, Mobility and Identities
vol. 21, 2019, 352 pp., 39,90€, br., ISBN 978-3-643-91093-6

Klaus Roth; Milena Benovska (Eds.)
Balkan Life Courses
Part 1: Childhood, Youth, Old Age, Work and Rituals
vol. 20, 2018, 314 pp., 39,90€, br., ISBN 978-3-643-91026-4

Klaus Roth; Asker Kartarı (eds.)
Cultures of Crisis in Southeast Europe
Part 2: Crises Related to Natural Disasters, to Spaces and Places, and to Identities
vol. 19, 2017, 368 pp., 39,90€, br., ISBN 978-3-643-90791-2

Klaus Roth; Asker Kartarı (eds.)
Cultures of Crisis in Southeast Europe
Part 1: Crises Related to Migration, Transformation, Politics, Religion, and Labour
vol. 18, 2016, 410 pp., 39,90€, br., ISBN-978-3-643-90763-9

LIT Verlag Berlin – Münster – Wien – Zürich
www.lit-verlag.de